P9-BZL-935

# *THOUGHTS AFIELD*

Books by Harold E. Kohn

FEELING LOW?

THROUGH THE VALLEY

PATHWAYS TO UNDERSTANDING

THOUGHTS AFIELD

# Thoughts Afield

*Meditations through the Seasons*

BY

HARALD E. KOHN

*Illustrated with sixty-three drawings by the author*

WM. B. EERDMANS PUBLISHING CO., GRAND RAPIDS, MICH.

LIBRARY OF CONGRESS CATALOG CARD NUMBER 59-8749

PRINTED IN THE UNITED STATES OF AMERICA

*– Dedication –*

This book is dedicated
in fond and grateful memory
to my father-in-law,
DR. JOHN SEYBERT DEABLER,
a good minister and friend.

*Prologue*

# A REASON FOR WRITING

More than five years have passed since first these weekly essays of mine began appearing in the *Charlevoix Courier,* and not once have I mentioned why they are printed there at all. Why does a person take time and spend effort confining in writing the vagrant thoughts that come and go while he is afield or recording the reflections that entertain him after he has returned to his fireside where he reviews the day's adventures? Is it because writing is fun? Sometimes, but not always. Often it is plain drudgery, especially when one is bone-tired from fishing or cutting brush or climbing hills. But there is simply no alternative to writing about an experience while it is fresh as early-evening air and as vibrantly alive and full as a whippoorwill's call.

Does a person write because he is unusually skillful at handling words? Not necessarily. At least the writer himself is never satisfied with his compositions and often brutally assails himself for what he has allowed to go to print. And it would be as accurate to say that a man is skilled because he writes as it is to declare he writes because he is skilled. Indeed a person must do some writing before he can know whether or not he has "the art." Robert Benchley once said, "It took me fifteen years to discover I had no talent for writing, but I couldn't give it up because by that time I was too famous."

Is money the chief motive for writing? Well, hardly! Thousands of books are published in America each year and only an armful are "best sellers" and big money makers. Many of the authors could have earned more money per hour hauling offal and trash in Chicago at the current hourly wage paid garbage collectors.

Is it the desire to create? Possibly. A search for prestige? That urge may prompt some writers. There are as many shades of motivation for writing as there are authors. But wherever writing is an art, rather than a mere trade, this basic impulse is certain to underlie all the rest — the *desire for sharing* the fruits of one's thought.

Writing is somewhat like sculpturing, painting, and composing music. They spring not from the creative impulse alone but from the desire to share with one's friends and with an ever-widening circle of one's kind the good that has come into one's own life. The sculptor molds a form to be seen by eyes other than his own. He does not hide his finished statue in a closet, taking an occasional affectionate glimpse for his own enjoyment. The sculptor shares with others the work of his hands. The painter intends that the product of his imagination and brush will be appreciated by other minds. The composer of a violin adagio hopes it will be played from many a concert stage by skilled and sensitive artists, so that other hearts may thrill in response to the melodies that first danced in the composer's brain. Writing, like sculpturing, painting, and composing music, may seek to give permanence to a transient thought or mood. But it does more. It aims to share that thought or mood with as many receptive people as possible. Like all the other arts, writing is a share-the-wealth program.

Henry David Thoreau once said, "To enjoy a thing exclusively is to exclude yourself from the true enjoyment of it." He would have understood the feelings of a certain lady of modest circumstances who was peacefully doing the week's mending when a telegram arrived informing her that a distant cousin had left her sole heir to his half-million-dollar estate. Much of the thrill of such news is in telling others about it, and the little lady dropped her mending, rushed to the telephone, and cried, "Hello, operator! Operator! Quick, get me anybody!"

Some such urgency to share is fundamental to sculpturing, painting, composing, writing, preaching — and all the other arts. If the essays in this series come within shouting distance of "the arts" it is because they are motivated by the desire to share with anyone who pauses to read them some quiet and reflective moments I have spent afield. The brief essays appearing in this book do not pretend to treat any subject exhaustively. They are what their collective title suggests them to be — *Thoughts Afield*: such meditations upon life's major and minor meanings as have been excited by a kill-deer's wild, plaintive cry in springtime, the sight of spotted fawns bounding through a fern-carpeted forest glade at twilight on a summer's day, the distant piping voices of migrating warblers on a frosty autumn night, or the vast silence of a cedar thicket on a wintry day when soft snow-flakes swirl and spiral soundlessly to earth, tenderly spreading an extra blanket over the sleeping Northland.

These reflections, once mine, I now share with you because I believe the stingiest hoarding of all is not that of collecting and concealing money, but that of hiding joy and inspiration. What I have is yours.

May you enjoy your share as I have mine.

*Acknowledgments*

To William B. Eerdmans, Sr., and Jr., who somehow always make the publishing of a book more of a joyous adventure than a business transaction

To Harold Totten, editor of the *Charlevoix Courier* where these essays first appeared, and to his staff for many kindnesses extended to me and for their faithful support of this joint venture in writing

To my partner in the ministry, the Reverend A. R. Gold, a seasoned servant of God and a wise and good friend who has given me unceasing help in our common tasks and constant encouragement in this writing ministry

To members and friends of the First Congregational Church of Charlevoix, and to all the people of our beloved town who have expressed a cordial interest in and a heartening response to these articles when they first appeared in print

To the many distracted and troubled souls from near and far who have in personal consultation, telephone call, and letter appealed for help, and whose welfare has made inevitable the applications of these "thoughts afield" to everyday human problems

*and most of all*

To my wife, Marian, and daughter, Carolyn, ideal companions whether afield or at home, for many hours of their inspiring, stimulating, and profoundly satisfying company.

*Contents*

# *SPRINGTIME THOUGHTS*

## *One*

# WHAT FOR?

THE KILLDEERS on our beaches are ready to nest now, but they will make no elaborate preparations for their family. A few stones will be scraped together for a nest, and there the female will lay about four buff-white eggs with chocolate-brown spots, about one and one-half by one and one-tenth inches in size — unusually large eggs for so small a bird. There is a reason for this size of the eggs. It is because killdeer babies are hatched on the ground in the midst of danger and must be in an advanced state of development when born into the world so that they can run from their enemies and hunt for their own food almost from the moment they emerge from their shells. A big egg is necessary to hold the advanced, precocious, bright-eyed, down-covered killdeer baby — a larger egg than is required for a baby robin, which is naked, blind, and altogether helpless when hatched. It is no mere happenstance that killdeers, which are robin-size, lay larger eggs than their red-breasted cousins do. There is a purpose in it, as there is for everything that occurs in nature.

Why is a woodcock's long bill hinged on the upper mandible? For a purpose — to permit him to open the end of his bill after the entire instrument has been buried deep into the moist earth. Then he can grip an earthworm and pull it to the surface.

What are earthworms for? They aerate the soil and make it fecund.

What purpose does a crab or crayfish serve? They are the garbage men of ponds and lakes and streams, scavengers that keep the under-water realms clean, as do the snails.

One of the barest essentials for understanding nature is to know that everything has a purpose. Nothing merely exists. Everything exists for a reason, and to know the reason is the beginning of natural wisdom.

An expression commonly heard these days is, "A fellow has to live, doesn't he?" An employee approaches his boss, asking for a raise in pay, and his employer wants to know why he should receive an increase. The man cites the rising cost of living, his growing family, and declares that money does not go as far as it once did, and finally he adds, "A fellow has to live, doesn't he?"

Or, a young man is changing his profession. After obtaining a good education he has worked at a low-paid position for the Federal Government's Fish and Wildlife Service. Now he decides to go into industry and try to become a highly paid executive. When he is asked if he does not like his work as a government biologist he answers, "Yes, very much!" Are his employers good to him? Do they treat him decently? Certainly! He could not wish for better employers. Why make a change then? "A fellow has to live, doesn't he?"

Doubtlessly, at some time or another you have used this expression, "A fellow has to live!" What would be your reply if someone countered with the question, "What for?" Would you be lost for an answer? Squelched? Why does a fellow have to live? What for? To what purpose?

The most fundamental explanation of anything is the purpose it serves, and no one understands much about anything unless he knows its purpose. A person who knew all about automobiles excepting the fact that they are made to ride in would be mighty stupid about them. A person who knew about the printing and binding of books and still did not understand that books are to be read would lack an elemental understanding of books. Anyone who knows all about high-school and college curricula, diplomas and degrees, and still is ignorant about the purpose of education is grossly uninformed about education.

An old grandmother entered a hardware store and declared she wanted to purchase a new stove for her living room. The salesman let loose a veritable barrage of sales patter about his latest-model heating stove. It had non-corroding bolts. It featured a newly patented insulating material. Just look at the gauge steel used in the jacket! Manipulate those clever controls! See the ample combustion chambers! All these gadgets, conveniences, and improvements were overwhelmingly convincing, the salesman thought, and he finished

his sales talk with a flourish, expecting an immediate and favorable response. But the old lady just looked at him, evidently expecting him to say more.

Taken back, the salesman said, somewhat stuffily, "Well, Madam, I've told you everything there is to know about that stove. Do you have any questions?"

"Yes, just one," she answered. "Will it keep an old lady warm?"

The most fundamental question that could be asked about a stove is, "Will it keep a person warm?" That is what a heating stove is for.

We need to ask such elemental questions these days about life in our world.

Those responsible for the education of our young might well look at our colleges and universities where there is an ever growing list of easy courses in such subjects as folk-dancing and fly-fishing and ask, "But does this system of education teach the young how to think and present them with a high standard of values? Do our educational institutions see that this generation's live wires are well grounded?" We have better school buildings now than the world has ever seen. What for?

People who are building bigger, more beautiful houses than have ever before been found on the earth should ask, "But will the house be a home, built of loving deeds as well as of brick, stone, mortar, and wood?" Better houses—what for?

Members of a cathedral-like church with a big budget, an impressive staff of ministers, and highly organized ecclesiastical machinery might well ask, "But does it lead people to a vital relationship with God?"

Many magazine articles and books are being written now about "how to relax" and "how to find peace of mind." But why relax? Why have peace of mind? To what good use will you put your relaxed body and peaceful mind? Most of the pundits never ask that question – or answer it. Happiness is not a matter of relaxation, or tranquil mind, but a state of going somewhere, earnestly, wholeheartedly, with undivided attention and devotion. Profound happiness and purposefulness are inseparable. Relaxation? Peace of mind? What for?

We are living longer than the people of any other generation in the world's history. Children born in America today have a life expectancy of approximately seventy years, more than twice the expectancy of youngsters born in Christ's time. And modern advances in science are pushing our longevity toward one hundred years. It may be good to live longer. It is far more important to live better. Longer lives – what for?

Saint Bernard of Clairvaux placed over his door the inscription: "Bernard, why are you here?" so that every time he entered his room he had to face anew the central purpose of his life.

It is a good question to hang above the opening of every day: "Why are you here?"

A fellow has to live, doesn't he? What for?

## *Two*

# ENJOY YOUR FAITH

FOR SOME YEARS now, I have been deeply interested in problems nature presents to curious minds. What is it, exactly, that makes deer change their coats from the grayish-brown garb of winter to the reddish-brown cloak of spring and summer? The lengthening days may trigger the transition, but what body chemistry decides the color? How do migrating birds find their way from Central and South America to a certain forty-acre plot in Hayes Township, Charlevoix County, State of Michigan, in the United States of America? What determines whether a newly born animal will be male or female? What is life? We know what life does, how it functions, but what is life itself? If death in man is the separation of soul from body, then what is death in a red fox, in a scarlet tanager, in a speckled trout? In humans there is something vital in the creature one moment and it is gone the next, and we say, "He is dead!" But what happens in death in non-humans? Why do thousands of gossamer spiders make a massive migration on silken parachutes on autumn days? Why are some of the lower animals color-blind while others are not? Why? Why? Why?

There exists a real temptation to be academic concerning nature, to spend one's nature study hours among heavy natural history textbooks and journals, seeking what the most authoritative scientists have to say about those problems. But if that is done, one misses the most important aspect of nature study – the exposure of one's eyes to beauty, the inhaling of evergreen-scented air, the feel of rough bark under one's finger tips and the softness of a pine-needle-carpeted forest aisle under foot and the soft caress of a lake breeze across one's face. The well-balanced student of nature is one who recognizes the problems of his field of interest and works toward their solution, but in the meantime he *experiences* nature directly, living it, breathing it, rejoicing in it.

This balance between recognizing the problems of life and

exploring its joys is a secret of achieving happiness. If we do not weigh the problems at all we become jittery activists or empty-headed sentimentalists, and if we consider only the problems we become burdened by discouragement and pessimism. The most satisfying attitude is to face the problem of a situation realistically while wringing from it the most possible good.

Employment offers problems of placement, wages, hours, fringe benefits, future advancements, getting along with employers and other employees and with the public, but there comes a time to quit weighing the problems and go to work and make the most of your job.

Love and marriage present problems. When we love deeply we accept a vulnerability to hurt which love always imposes. Those whom we love most have a capacity to inflict upon us the most painful suffering. Their praise is our highest encouragement, but their criticisms are most profoundly discomforting. Their presence is most satisfying, but their departure is most agonizing. Their life with us is most treasured, but their death is most soul-wrenching. Yet we love, and most of us have been loved into being.

One of the chief reasons more people are not happy in their religious faith is that they are too absorbed by the problems of religion and too lax concerning the practice of the religious life. We think we are being religious when we debate the existence of God and come to some positive conclusion that there really is an Infinite Being. Or we feel we have had a basic experience of faith when we have attempted to harmonize the existence of a good God with the fact of suffering in His world. Again, we raise the question of how God can give any attention to this tiny speck of a planet and its inhabitants when He has millions of bigger celestial bodies to keep in their orbits and supervise. Or we wonder how our finite minds can have any relationship with an Infinite Creator. So we add up the issues and call the sum total "the problem of God."

But God is vastly more than a problem to consider. He is a Resource of power to be drawn upon, the Giver of gifts to be thanked, the Redeemer whose forgiveness we can experi-

ence, a Companion who accompanies us on life's travels, a Presence to be enjoyed.

The Bible is a book with problems. The books of the Bible were not written by scientists as scientific texts, and so they present some conclusions that are at variance with scientific findings. We cannot be certain whose pen was used in writing some of the chapters and books, or exactly when some books were written. The Old Testament conception of God and the New Testament portrayal of God are difficult to harmonize. Some of the heroes and heroines of the Bible had low ethical and moral standards for which they would be jailed today. Numberless such problems arise in some people's minds when the Bible is mentioned.

But the person who sees the Bible primarily as a book of problems, or even as a book that needs argumentative defense, does not really know the Bible. This is the Book that has inspired our best literature, art, and music. It is the most candid of books, picturing us as we are. But it is also a hopeful Book, showing us what we might be with God's help. The New Testament is the world's most joyous Book, opening with the coming of the Savior and drawing near a close with a glad shout of victory that "the Lord God omnipotent reigneth." There are problems in the Bible, all right, but revelation, profound insight, and immense hope are there, too. Although no man understands all the Bible, everyone can understand enough to live better than he is now living. To anyone who will read it the Bible is a book of spiritual adventure, with heights to climb, depths to plumb, sunlit stretches of revelation to visit, experiences men of old have had with God that we could well repeat, standards like those of the Sermon on the Mount we should stretch to reach.

Voltaire, considering that the Bible was outdated, one time said that in one hundred years the Bible would be a forgotten book, found only in museums. When the hundred years were up, Voltaire's own home was occupied by the Geneva Bible Society, and the Bible was being read by more people than ever before. The Bible still lives because, in spite of its problems, it speaks to our condition and answers our spiritual needs.

Prayer, too, is problematical. Why pray if God is all-wise, knowing our needs better than we do, and all-good, giving us what is best for us regardless of our asking? Moreover, if this world is run by invincible laws, how can prayer change anything? Why does God so often answer "No" or "Wait a while"? How dare we try to communicate with God when He is so good and we are such blunderers, when He is so wise and we are so foolish? These and many more problems assault our minds, demanding answers. And there are answers, if we have the courage to look for them. But prayer is more than a problem to be pondered or discussed. Prayer is primarily a privilege we enjoy. No one knows much about prayer until he prays, and the best way to know more about prayer is to pray more often and more meaningfully. I have felt about some discussions I have heard on prayer as Walt Whitman did about a lecture on astronomy—

"When I heard the learn'd astronomer,
When the proofs, the figures, were ranged in columns before me,
When I was shown the charts and diagrams, to add, divide, and measure them,
When I, sitting, heard the astronomer where he lectured with much applause in the lecture-room,
How soon unaccountable I became tired and sick,
Till rising and gliding out, I wandered off by myself;
In the mystical moist night air, and from time to time,
Looked up in perfect silence at the stars."

Religious questions deserve a careful consideration, and an alert and devout mind will continue to seek answers to life's perplexing riddles. But the quest is perilous to a person's spiritual welfare if it becomes a substitute for enjoying one's faith. To refrain from experiencing religion while we weigh its problems is like a meteorologist studying the atmosphere with weather balloons, weather maps, charts, and all sorts of delicate instruments that result in carefully worked-out calculations, but in the meantime holding his breath until all the data are collected. His very study will be the death of him. While he studies the atmosphere he had better breathe it,

too, if he wants to stay alive. Religious faith is worth studying, but it is primarily for breathing!

Well, that's all for now. For a few minutes I'm going to cease thinking about the problems of nature and God, lay down this pen, step out into the woods and breathe the good clean air, and walk around a bit, lost in the Incomparable Companionship.

*Three*

# BIG - HEARTEDNESS

THE EARTH has begun to respond to spring. From our front windows at Wide Sky Harbor we watch the slow breaking and melting of Lake Charlevoix ice. Wide cracks appear around the old offshore pilings, and a large pool of open water has begun to form there. Any day or any moment now American goldeneye ducks and buffleheads will make their first spring visit to this bay, gliding in over woods that fringe the lake and landing in a fine spray of chill water. There they will swim and preen their feathers and converse in a low, confidential duck manner.

The soil, as well as the lake, is coming to life, a sleeping beauty awakening to the kiss of spring sunshine and the caresses of warm winds. Soon the air will be faintly scented with spring flowers and freshly plowed soil. Trilliums will nod at our woods edge, as they have bowed in greeting to the advent of spring each year since long before the first plow split Michigan earth in preparation for the white man's crops. Golden bees will drone from one fragrant blossom to another. Everywhere in the Northland, lake and lake shore, open meadow and deep forest will feel the gentle grace of the shining sun, and every place will respond with its own peculiar zest and beauty.

As winter retreats to the far North and spring comes on we become more aware of the magnanimity of Nature, a sort of elemental big-heartedness and inclusive impartiality that is a reflection of the character of God. Spring sunshine will not fall on beautiful, graceful birch trees alone, but upon the less lovable scrub pine, alders, and willows, too. April showers will not pick and choose, playing favorites with the daffodils and crocuses, and shunning objectionable dandelions and lowly violets, blessing the arbutus and avoiding the bloodroot and wild strawberry. The great sun will warm the acres of saint and sinner alike. Warm rains will beat with equal benefit upon the gardens of the grateful and the grumbling.

Nature's inclusiveness is a reminder of the great-heartedness of God, who cares for those who love Him and for those who are indifferent to Him, who has room in His attention and concern for those who praise Him and for those who lightly use His name. As Jesus put it, "He makes his sun rise on the evil and the good, and sends rain on the just and unjust."

This is one meaning of Godlikeness – caring for people who do not care for you, loving those who hate you, doing what you can to help those who would do all they could to hurt you.

Perhaps the nineteenth-century American preacher Henry Ward Beecher was no thoroughgoing saint, as some recent biographers have hinted, but he did possess this grace of magnanimity. He treated his enemies as kindly as he did his friends. One man in Brooklyn once detested Beecher with a hot and bitter hatred. But later he became one of Beecher's most devoted admirers. He explained his change of heart by saying that whenever anyone did anything to hurt Henry Ward Beecher, the great orator was miserable until he had done that enemy a good turn. The word was passed around Brooklyn: "If you want a favor from Beecher, kick him!"

Henry Ward Beecher illustrated in his life a little of the spirit that motivated Jesus. When a person abused the Master, He saw the wrong as a sign of some deep need in the man's life. His attention was on His enemy's welfare rather than on His own hurt. Wherever that attitude is found it is a mark of godliness.

Springtime would be an appropriate time to get some of this magnanimity of Nature and this greatness of God into our living. You must know someone upon whom you can start using it.

*Four*

# BETWEEN TIMES

ALTHOUGH the first robin of springtime brings excitement to the North Country, every newspaper vying with every other one to report the sight of the earliest red-breasted visitor, the robin that interests me most is not spring's first newcomer. Far more impressive, to my notion, are robins seen or heard later in the year. Often when walking through dense cedar swamps in late summer or early fall, I've been aware of a silent presence haunting the deep shadows. Then the faint whirr of ghostly wings draws my attention to the spectral form of a robin spiriting itself away amidst cedar boughs. No shrieking protest is made at a human being's blundering invasion of its sanctuary. Never a chirp nor a cheery warble. There is something about these robins seen between springs that reminds me of the "strong, silent men" our pioneering fathers were. These birds haunt me. I love them.

Then there are the hardy robins that refuse to go south when fall comes, and the air chills and snowflakes fall. Instead, seeking out thick plantings of cedar trees or pines and a generous supply of the berries of hawthorn, juniper, sumac, and bayberry, they remain in the North. They may migrate slightly southward, say from the tree limits of Alaska to northern Michigan, or from Newfoundland to New Jersey — just enough to qualify as migrating birds — but go south to the Gulf Coast, or to North Carolina, or to Florida with their warm-blooded red-breasted brothers? No, sir! They will winter where winter is worthy of its name. So, in the coldest weather, in the thickest growth of cedar and pine, robins can occasionally be seen. And the bright flicker of a robin amidst snow-laden swamp thickets is a quickening sight!

But the robin that pleases me most is the zestful songster that awakens me from sleep on a spring morning at Hidden Brook, splitting the darkness with his chisel-sharp notes, letting the light of a new day drift down upon the earth. He isn't the first robin of spring. He's just another robin, in high

good spirits. But as his song floats down from the ancient apple tree on the pasture's edge, I thank the Creator for this cocky little herald of a new day.

A person's enthusiasm for bird life can hardly be measured by his thrill at seeing spring's first robin. Such a sight comes but once each year and is apt to impress even the most phlegmatic soul. A better gauge of one's bird-watching fervor is what a person notices between springs — the hundredth robin as well as the first. In fact, a good way of assessing anyone's ardor for anything is by testing that person's fascination for it *between* exciting events. Just about anyone can show an interest in trout fishing if the big ones are striking every time his lure hits the water. The real trout fisherman is one whose enthusiasm is sustained when hour after hour he doesn't see a sign of a trout. In the long stretches between strikes he is still a trout fisherman.

Often we read in our newspapers about some medal-winning soldier who proved himself a hero during the war, now being imprisoned for theft, forgery, embezzlement, criminal assault, or any number of crimes. When war demanded a rare, big show of spirit, he had it, and became a hero. But he lacked the sustained strength to carry him through less eventful days.

Almost any young man's eye is apt to be caught by a "cute kid," a good figure, a gay demeanor, dancing eyes, peaches-and-cream complexion, and laughter as lovely as a thrush's song. Fascination may grow to delirium, and even to marriage. Courtship is hardly a fair test of the depth of a young man's feeling. If he wants her, he is almost certain to be good to her. But after marriage — ten years after marriage — then what? Does he remember wedding anniversaries and her birthdays? Even that isn't enough. How thoughtful is he *between* the great events? Does he show the little courtesies, daily? Are there frequent evidences of tenderness? How do married couples act toward each other between the great moments? That is the final test of marriage happiness.

It doesn't take much of a Christian to attend church on Christmas or Easter, when the atmosphere is bright with religious excitement, or on some Sunday when a world-renowned, spell-binding guest preacher happens to be in the pulpit. Your real loyalty is shown when Sunday morning is rainy, and bed feels soft and good, and a thought like "I can hear that preacher any time" stirs lazily in your mind. The really memorable religious experiences come infrequently and are hardly an accurate measure of one's spirituality. A better test is your religious conduct between the great events.

Look back over your life to the big, stirring, eventful days. They haven't occurred often, have they? They come about as frequently as the spring's first robin. Thus they hardly afford you a reliable test of what you are. A better gauge is how you handle less momentous occasions, what you do with the between-time, common days.

*Five*

# INCOME AND EXPENDITURE

THE LARGEST TRILLIUM I've ever seen is growing in our woods. There may be larger ones somewhere in the North, but this white blossom, five and one-half inches wide, excells all I have seen in the wild. The plant stands on a slope near the back of our acreage, silhouetted against a tree trunk and nestled amidst a cluster of other flowers of its kind. The soil there is moist enough to suit these lovely perennials and rich in humus so that all the blossoms are of generous size, but the dimensions of this single bloom signify unusual vitality and the most ideal conditions of light and shade, moisture and mild acidity of the soil, and high fertility of the earth.

After looking long and appreciatively at this large and lovely specimen of *trillium grandiflorum*, I began wondering why this particular blossom was so much larger than its sister flowers which surround it. Why its unusual growth? Then I recalled an old principle of biological growth: the primal condition of organic growth is a surplus of income over expenditure. All living tissue in time breaks down. It happens in deer, in trees, in shrubs, in human beings, in the trillium, and in all other creatures. A growing body, like a growing bank account, is possible only when deposits exceed withdrawals. This particular trillium, resting at the foot of a sheltering tree, protected from buffeting winds, rooted in highly organic soil, must have found unusual resources that enabled it to stretch higher and broader than its fellows, and to keep on growing after they had reached maturity.

What is true of the trillium is true of all creation. No creature in all the universe, from the microscopic one-celled amoeba to the six-ton African elephant and the six-thousand-ton Big Tree of Central California, exists or grows by will-power alone. All organisms succeed in staying alive only by assimilating resources from outside themselves, and they grow only when the income of these resources exceeds the expenditure of energy.

In these days when nervous exhaustion is such a common-place experience, when the rate of mental breakdowns has soared to new heights and we have run out of room to house and feed those who can no longer cope with the problems of everyday life and need institutional care – in these times of numerous and extravagant demands upon our intellectual, moral and spiritual strength – look to your resources! If you want to stay alive see that your resources *match* your expenditures. If you want to grow see that your income *exceeds* your outgo.

The law of organic sustenance is also the rule of mental and moral development. Mental and spiritual growth results from absorbing more information, meaning, truth, beauty, and goodness than one can possibly spend. Eyes and ears, and our other organs of sense, compose a small reception committee that invites into our inner life the beauties of sunrises and sunsets, far-off stars, laughing voices, stirring music, words of wisdom and inspiration such as we find in the Holy Bible and the stimulating stories of heroic living found in the biographies of the leaders of the race. With these receptors we gather in the influences of worship, fellowship with friends, wholesome play, and all the happiest experiences of our lives. These things represent the good income of our lives, the nourishment that feeds our minds and enlarges our souls. Without an income of goodness we cannot spend ourselves doing good, improving our community, cooperating with God in making His world a fit home for His children. The capacity to suffer without bitterness, to endure disappointment without loss of hope, to withstand strain without grumbling is a matter of being able to *afford* these things, knowing that we can spend energy and thought, concern and strength upon them endlessly, if need be. A great faith comes to the person who is confident that he cannot exhaust the resources that God has placed here for our use. He knows that he is surrounded with power in the person of parents, brother or sister, friends, and fellow workers. He is aware that the Presence of God is as much around and within him as is the air he beathes. He draws strength from God as readily, as unconsciously, and as constantly, as he replenishes his breath from the atmosphere.

Nothing shows more plainly what we are and how we have been fed than does a crisis. Then, like a starved deer chased by dogs, the malnourished soul falters while the healthy one relies upon hidden stores of stamina. Like a plant set in drought-ridden soil, the unresourceful soul withers, but the good one sends roots down deeper to secret springs. A sudden bereavement, loss of health, a period of unemployment, harsh criticism, a violent disagreement, or any of a vast range of emergencies show how our spirits have been fed.

At our best we are people with inexhaustible resources, like a light bulb attached to a huge power station, like a faucet connected to Lake Michigan, like a sheep in a great green pasture, like a trillium with rootage in rich forest soil.

*Six*

# TOO MUCH PREPARATION

ON THESE WARM days we see wild ducks flying rapidly over the bay, circling over the woods that fringe the lake, and returning to light upon the dancing waters. Greater scaup rest here on their way from salt water bays along the eastern seaboard of our country to the Arctic, where they will raise their young. American goldeneyes relax here and replenish their strength before they continue their flight from the coast of South Carolina to breeding grounds extending from Northern Michigan to Hudson Bay. The small and beautiful buffleheads find a breathing spell in this bay before they resume their travels to western Canada. Before summer arrives an occasional pair of ruddy ducks may drop in to see us, a great variety of other webfoots will quack and gabble here briefly before taking wing for distant ponds and streams, and the familiar mallards will paddle contentedly along our shores and possibly nest in our neighborhood.

One of the traits of the migrating birds that intrigue and inspire me is the spontaneity of their traveling. They make no long, involved, wearisome preparations. Their readiness for a journey is of a simple sort, compounded mainly of a strong body, much courage, deep urgency, and a sense of direction. Their modest preliminaries are as few and uncomplicated as those of John Muir, that great-hearted and self-reliant American naturalist, who said that all he needed to do in getting ready for a natural history expedition was to "throw some tea and bread in an old sack and jump over the back fence."

Migrating ducks could teach us a valuable lesson concerning our own life-adventures. What we need most for our travels through life is not a heap of gadgets, but a sense of direction, courage, and a willingness to move on and do the thing we feel a holy urge to do.

Too much preparation for a task is self-defeating. We can become so over-burdened with the fantastic details of getting

ready to do a thing that it never gets done. There is an old fable about a foolish knight of yore who prepared to make a long journey. He thought it wise to be ready for every emergency that might arise on his travels, so he put a mouse-trap in his pocket in case he should be troubled with mice. Just in case he might be annoyed by bees he hung a beehive over his shoulder. In the event that he should meet with hordes of mosquitoes along the way, and they should try to work through the joints in his armor and around his exposed eyes, he placed mosquito netting in his satchel. Because his armor might get dented, he carried a large repair kit. Anticipating that his horse might break its harness straps, the knight packed extra leather and mending tools. On and on, he added one precaution after another until his load was so great that he had to give up making the journey. The knight's dilemma is a human problem found among timid souls everywhere. We are prone to make such elaborate preparations for a task that the duty never gets performed.

We will visit a friend who is in trouble as soon as we can think of something appropriate and impressive to say. But by the time we have developed our pretty little speech the friend's heartache is over, or converted into bitterness, and our opportunity is gone.

We will write that letter of condolence, or gratitude, or sincere praise, when we have the time to compose a literary masterpiece, but the burden of such composition is so great that it is postponed indefinitely.

Life is so full of opportunities for which much preparation is absolutely essential – such as choice of profession, selecting a mate, building a home – that conscientious people are apt to make the mistake of undertaking *nothing* without long consideration and complex planning. We need to make room in our living for spontaneous acting upon good impulses. As Henry Amiel once said, "Life is short, and we have not much time for gladdening the hearts of those who are traveling the dark way with us. Oh, be swift to love! Make haste to be kind!"

*Seven*

# BEAUTY AND BLEMISHES

On this early spring evening I spent a while among the trees at Hidden Brook. Leaving behind my favorite white birches, I gave special attention to a grove of hardwoods, the gnarled and venerable maples twisted with the infirmities of age, and senile beeches with swollen joints and gray skin. These ancient trees stand near enough to each other to whisper shy, breezy, woods-gossip about their animal neighbors, yet far enough apart to maintain the crotchety independence of old age.

In the quiet of this woodland I was aware once more that Nature need not be perfect to be beautiful or to accomplish her work. These trees bear all the marks of their dotage, broken limbs, hollows and holes here and there, bacteria and virus infections. Their troubles are not enough to destroy the health of the trees completely or to deface their beauty entirely. But the defects are there, reminders that even Nature is imperfect in her accomplishments.

Elsewhere at Hidden Brook other flaws appear. Here a marauding porcupine has girded a tamarack, killing the tree near the crown. Over there the deer have browsed some seedling maples too closely. Now they will never grow to maturity. The grasses here, as elsewhere across North America, are vulnerable to the attack of various grass diseases, one hundred and twenty-five species of rust afflicting nearly four hundred species of grasses in the United States. Moles make humps in the sod. Insects attack the leaves of spring flowers. Everywhere the discerning eye looks closely enough there is some blemish, some imperfection.

Still, all in all, the total impression these acres make upon the observer is one of unutterable beauty and total success — loveliness of color and form, of light and shade, and prosperity of tree, shrub, and flower, health of bird and beast and fish. Nature need not be perfect to be beautiful, successful, and useful.

One of the greatest deterrents of happiness and usefulness is a fanatical perfectionism. When a person cannot accept or enjoy anything short of perfection he dooms himself to wretchedness and habitually condemns those near him by his disapproval and carping criticism.

One would think that the perfectionists, with their high ideals, would be God's chosen people and the cream of any community. But they are not. As a rule they are bane rather than blessing, wherever they are found.

Here is Frank for an example – a dyed-in-the-wool perfectionist. (Frank is not from our town, so there's no use in trying to identify him!) He has tried all sorts of jobs, but none exactly suits his talents, and he will not compromise by taking anything less than the ideal situation. Of course, many kinds of employment have seemed ideal on the day he was hired, but before long some flaw appeared. Sometimes the employer was cranky. Again, raises did not come frequently enough. The hours were too long. People were unappreciative. Frank moved from job to job and from town to town until his wife tearfully complained that she never lived in a place she could call home for long.

The churches did not suit Frank either. Some did not "preach the true gospel." Others did not elect him to high office. One was not friendly enough. Another's revival meetings were not as fervid as Frank thought they should be.

So Frank has moved constantly on, from town to town, from job to job, from church to church, forever seeking a perfection that he has never found. His life has been one disappointment after another, and he has dragged his wife and four children with him on his futile quest for a model town, a faultless job, and a perfect church.

Yet some people have remained in the towns from which Frank fled and have improved them with their presence. Someone has taken every task Frank quit and has made a success of it. Someone has worshipped and worked in every church Frank has deserted and has helped make it God's instrument for good in the community.

The perfectionist is more to be pitied than blamed, for he is the tragic victim of his own unrealistic, rigid standards.

·HK·

He panics when he makes a mistake and cudgels himself with self-recriminations whenever his morbid self-examination reveals the slightest defect. He drives relentlessly for faultlessness in his friends and withholds wholehearted affection and high regard from those who do not exactly conform to his own standards (although the one perfect Man loved the rankest sinner). He possesses feelings of superiority over those who have not achieved his own high level of moral and intellectual attainment, but sometimes succeeds in hiding these feelings behind a polished mask of friendliness. Still, he is torn between his inner unfriendliness and his attempt to be outwardly gracious.

One of the perfectionist's chief difficulties is dissipation of his energies. If he is a businessman who dabbles in politics and owns his own home and heads a family and plays golf, his attempting perfection in business, in political achievement, in caring for house and yard, in functioning as husband and father, and in the game of golf pulls him too hard in too many directions, and since his neurotic pride will not let him be satisfied with less than a perfect performance in any area, he is constantly frustrated. He cannot bear failure. He cannot admit he is too weak to bear so heavy a load of activities. To acknowledge his strength is limited is unbearable. He is trapped among his multiform activities, his neurotic pride, and his unreasonable perfectionism.

The perfectionist can never enjoy anything on earth completely because the things of earth come with built-in blemishes, and it is the flaws that catch his attention and hold his interest. (Most of us have a little of this trait, but in the perfectionist it amounts to a zeal.) Draw a solid black circle, one inch in diameter on a square yard sheet of white paper and hold it up to an audience and ask the people what they see. The almost unanimous reply will be: "A black dot!" Yet the black dot occupies only a small fraction of the space on the paper. A more exact answer would be: "A large sheet of white paper with a small black dot." But we are accustomed to seeing the small black dots rather than the large white sheets, the little fault in a neighbor's life rather than the enormous amount of good that is there, the little hardships

of life rather than the abundant opportunities, small shadows rather than a flood of sunshine.

There is one kind of perfectionism that is wholesome rather than fault-finding, that is an incentive to better living rather than a barrier. The Master spoke of it when He said: "Be ye therefore perfect, even as your Father in heaven is perfect." By that He did not mean that in this life we can be as flawless as God is. Where Matthew used the word "perfect" Luke translated it "merciful." We are to be as lacking in vengefulness as God is, Godlike in our readiness to forgive. While one cannot be utterly perfect in all things (which the perfectionist aims for and insists all his acquaintances achieve), we can seek for Godlike excellence at one specific point – in magnanimity, being as big-hearted in dealing with the children of earth as God is. And that is a big enough order to keep all of us busy, and striving, and humble.

KOHN

*Eight*

# EFFORT IS NOT ENOUGH

THE LAST PATCHES of snow are rapidly disappearing now as spring advances and the sun warms the ground. Much of the grass on our lawn has already turned green, and in a few places it has grown enough to give our rabbit neighbors cover as well as food. Insects are emerging from their hiding places. Chipmunks and skunks, snakes, toads, and frogs are awakening from winter sleep. Hepatica, trillium, and yellow lady-slippers will soon burst into bloom, and trees are tinged with the yellow-green cast of leaves that are on the verge of opening. Killdeers call along our shore, and migrating ducks can be seen from our front windows, dipping offshore, seeking a traveler's snack of minnows or crustaceans. Earth and air are replete with signs of renewal.

But the earth does not revive *itself* in spring. No inner effort and strain will suffice to bring flowers to bloom and draw the warblers northward. What is it, then, that unlocks the soil so that green grasses and bright, multi-colored flowers might come trooping forth?

Spring begins far away in outer space where whirls that golden star, the sun. From ninety million miles away the beneficent sun smiles upon the earth, sending down heat and light. As our earth spins around the sun, held by its tether of gravitational pull, this little satellite turns on its tilted axis at an oblique angle of 23½ degrees. In December, January, and February the Northern Hemisphere turns away from the sun and the Southern Hemisphere inclines toward it, while during June, July, and August this obliquity inclines our hemisphere toward the sun. Springtime is that in-between period when the earth is changing its position, turning the North toward our great source of heat and light, allowing the good influences of the sun to fall upon us and make all the changes we know as "springtime." Spring is that time when our hemisphere simply moves into the position where the sun can bestow its favors, and the sun does the rest.

One secret of successful and happy living is that of recognizing and employing the principle of placing yourself in the position where the best things can happen to you. Miracles of spiritual change can then take place which effort alone can never perform.

No worse advice could possibly be given to some people than, "Try! Try harder!" A person who suffers from chronic fatigue or strain, or one who has experienced shock knows full well that his efforts to improve himself are unavailing. Often much of his problem can be blamed on trying *too* hard. What he needs is not more effort but more resources, not more pressure on the accelerator but gas in the tank, not more fertilizer and hoeing, but more spring sunshine and rain.

Effort has its place in life and it has its limitations, too. Effort can get you to a concert on time, but it will not suffice to enjoy the music. Strain to listen, stretch to get every note and you will be miserable. But sit back with open mind and heart, as a field in springtime is open to the sky, and let the music fall upon you. Soak it in. Let it seep down into the roots of your being, and a good response will have a chance of flowering.

Effort will get you dressed, into your car, and to your friend's home for dinner and conversation, but effort alone will not make a pleasant evening. Try hard to impress your friend with your good will, your intelligence, your prestige, try hard to have a good time and you will ruin your evening. Friendship is enjoyed most when effort is least apparent, and when each participant is quietly absorbing the good in another's life, as the earth drinks in the warmth and light of the sun with effortless ease.

Effort will aid in following a doctor's orders concerning taking medicines regularly, following a rigid diet, getting sufficient rest or enough exercise. But effort itself will not heal. God heals, quietly, silently, through the recuperative powers He has stored in you, and with the aids provided by science, while you sleep, while you think of other matters besides health, and while you are not trying at all.

Effort will provide a time and place of prayer, but effort alone does not supply us fellowship with God. Some people conceive of prayer as the effort made to get God to listen to them and do their will. To them prayer is a matter of mastering the right vocabulary, learning the magical formula that will assault God at His weakest points and make Him give in to their whims. Such exertions are poor substitutes for meaningful prayer. Prayer is listening to God as well as talking to Him. It is thanking God as well as trying to get something from Him. Prayer is resting for a while in God's greatness.

Doing most things requires some effort, as when plowing and sowing seed. But the best things that ever happen to us do not come from effort alone, but from quiet, receptive waiting, too, as the earth now patiently waits for spring sun and rain to call the flowers out and bring the birds back home.

*Nine*

# CARRYING ON

WHEN I WAS a little lad, and one of the youngsters in our family or neighborhood would boisterously misbehave, I would hear some of the old folks exclaim, "How that kid carries on!" I never could discover the origins of that quaint, folksy expression, but I knew then and know now what they meant by "carry on." Children who "carry on" are making nuisances of themselves, getting into mischief, causing anxiety.

However, "carrying on" has a higher, larger meaning, too, and I am reminded of it as springtime brings manifold changes to the North. Birds are returning. Yesterday we saw our first killdeer of the season on our beach, and today a robin jauntily hopped across our front lawn. They have returned to these haunts for mating and rearing their young and "carrying on" their race.

A few days ago at Hidden Brook I saw in the crotch of an arthritic old apple tree the abandoned nest of a wood thrush. Perhaps the builders of that nest are dead now, but their offspring will be returning to the North within the next few weeks, and we shall hear their plaintive call, "Ah-oh-lee, oh-lee-lay, pee-dle-ee," ringing through our woods as their spot-breasted forebears have sung for ages, and we shall see them darting among the trees with building materials for their homes. They will be "carrying on," singing their ancestors' unfinished songs, bringing more small, winged carolers into the world, so that the music of the forests need not be forever stilled.

Last year's yellow lady-slippers and marsh marigolds have long since wilted, drooped, and died. But all along our brook bank there will appear this spring the descendants of last year's flowers, carrying a tradition of quiet beauty into a year the parent flowers will never see.

Springtime is courtship time, mating time, family time, blossom time, renewal and resurrection time, when all Nature is "carrying on."

One of the most powerful motives to be found in human hearts is the incentive to "carry on" for someone whose life's work is done. George Gipp, one of the greatest football players the game ever knew, died at twenty-three years of age. He had been a rugged, hard-hitting player on one of Knute Rockne's Notre Dame teams and was affectionately known to his teammates and to football fans across the nation as "the Gipper." When death was near, Knute Rockne was called to the hospital to see Gipp. Fumbling for words to say to the dying boy, Rockne bent over him and said, "It's pretty tough to go, isn't it, Gipp?"

The boy smiled and answered, "What's tough about it? I've no complaints." Then he added, "Rock, I've got to go, and it's all right, and I'm not afraid. I'll plunge into this game of dying as I did into West Point and Southern California. Sometimes, Rock, when the going is rough and everything goes wrong, and our team isn't getting a break, tell our boys to go in there with all they've got and win one game – just one game – for 'the Gipper.' Rock, I don't know exactly where I'll be, but I'll know about it. I'll be watching from somewhere. You can count on that."

Two years passed. Notre Dame's football team experienced a difficult season. Many boys suffered from injuries, and the team's spirit was low. Then came the Army game, the Gipper's favorite, and the hardest game of the year. At the end of the first half both teams were scoreless.

Between halves Knute Rockne talked quietly to the nearly demoralized team. He told them about his hospital call on George Gipp during that football hero's last days. He relayed to them the dying wish of the great athlete — "Win one game, just one, for 'the Gipper.'" The boys were hushed, reverent, and inwardly moved.

At the beginning of the last half they ran out on the field and, as the sports writers put it, "seemed inspired, exalted, overpowering." After a few minutes of play, with sweeping end runs and precise forward passes, Notre Dame was within striking distance of its goal. Chevigny was given the ball and bulldozed his way through Army for the winning touchdown. As Chevigny pawed his way out of the heap of players who had fallen over him, he smiled and said, "Boys, that's one for the old Gipper." Notre Dame had "carried on" for George Gipp.

There is a unique, incomparable satisfaction in feeling joined to those who have gone on before us, so that their work cannot die but continues to find expression through us. I know from experience. My father-in-law, Dr. John S. Deabler, was a splendid minister of the gospel and served more than forty years among Michigan churches, preaching, comforting the bereaved, bringing hope and reassurance to the sick and wise counselling to the problem-ridden. Then one night a telephone call brought us the news that he had died suddenly of a heart attack. He had preached only a few days before and planned to preach again and again. He hoped to call on the needy and help the distressed for some years to come. He died in the midst of much he still wanted to do. Even now, fourteen years after his going, there are occasions when I leave the pulpit, a hospital room, or a consultation, thinking to myself with a glad sense of privilege, "That's one for Dad Deabler." It is gratifying to be able to "carry on" for someone like Dad.

Patriotism is a kind of "carrying on," a persistence in bearing the highest, noblest aims of the founding fathers of our nation into eras they could not enter and applying their insight, wisdom, courage, and selfless concern for the public welfare to present-day problems. It is a willingness to sacrifice for our country's good in our time as our fathers did in their day.

One could say nothing better about a modern-day disciple of Christ than, "See how that fellow carries on!" Isn't that what Jesus expected of those devoted to Him – that they would be extensions of Himself, walking where His feet had never trod, speaking His words in languages His lips never uttered, using instruments of mercy His hands never touched? How else could one interpret His saying, "He who believes in me will also do the works that I do: and greater works than these will he do, because I go to the Father." A disciple of Christ can be defined in many ways, but my choicest definition is, "A disciple of Christ is one who carries on for Him."

How have you been "carrying on"?

# *SUMMERTIME THOUGHTS*

*Ten*

# WHAT IS BEAUTY?

IN NATURE beauty never exists for beauty's sake. Rather, loveliness is always a by-product of some other things Nature is trying to accomplish.

Natural beauty is often an expression of the vigor of living things and of their resolute endeavor to find food, to mate and rear their young, and to escape their enemies. A swan demonstrates such a charm. Among the loveliest creatures to be found in all creation are the European and Asiatic mute swans (now naturalized in America), the large and magnificent American trumpeter swan and the American whistling swan. Besides its startling, conspicuous whiteness, the swan's most famous physical feature is its curved neck. In all the wide, wild world no more graceful curve can be found than in the long arched neck of this elegant bird. But the beauty of the swan's curved neck is a mere incidental. The neck is long so that the bird can feed upon the bottom of shallow waters where it finds its favorite food without the necessity of diving. Why is the neck held in a loose "S"-shape, rather than rigidly straight like a stick? Because it is more comfortable that way! A swan's graceful beauty is thus an expression of its pursuit of food and its search for an effortless way of carrying its long appendage.

The male scarlet tanager's gay red and black uniform is designed to attract the eyes of its mate. Attractiveness is an outgrowth of usefulness. A whitetail deer's bounding grace is beautiful to behold, but beauty is not its goal. Escape is its aim. Look behind the loveliness in nature, and you are apt to find some practical purpose from which beauty is an offshoot, a by-product.

Again, beauty is an expression of orderliness in nature as seen in the regularity of spaces between waves on an ocean, ripples on a pond, growth marks on a shell or cross marks on a hawk's lost feather, or the infinite variations on the hexagonal theme that we observe in snowflakes.

Beauty may also be a revelation of harmony in nature. Man sometimes mixes his colors in weird and jarring discord, wearing a bright red tie over a vividly purple shirt, and his wife may break all known laws of color-concord by sporting a lemon-yellow blouse next to a burnt-orange skirt. But Nature tends to smooth out the dissension between colors, so that no matter how many hues appear in a sunset they never clash. Regardless of the varied coloring in a field of fall flowers there occurs no shocking dissidence. Beauty is there because harmony is present. They go hand in hand.

Americans are a beauty-conscious people. We find an age-old delight in butterflies in flight, starlit nights, a choir's singing, a ship in sail, a child's smile, the wrinkled parchment of an aged face. Beauty in music and art and literature touches us and inspires us as it has our forebears. But in addition we are influenced by unending propaganda from cosmetic companies, tooth-paste corporations, hair-oil syndicates and corset foundations, all seeking to assure us that beauty can be ours if we but apply their product. Beauty, they teach, is something to be directly sought after and applied from the outside. It isn't.

Real beauty is a by-product found while seeking something else. In nature's wild creatures and in man it is incidental to a way of life and is an expression of an inner condition, not an application of something from outside, like rouge on a pale and sallow face.

The beauty of Lincoln's life was an expression of his integrity, his desire to save the Union, his compassion for his enemies. He didn't intend that his character would be splendorous. He wanted only that it should be sound and magnanimous. But in building these virtues he unintentionally established beauty in his life as well.

St. Francis of Assisi had no intention of developing a radiant character. The splendor of his personality was an outgrowth of the way he lived. Denying inherited riches and dressing himself in rags, he cast his lot with the poor, the sick, and distressed. More than seven hundred years after his death, the luster of his goodness still illumines and blesses us.

In addition to being a consequence of good behavior, beautiful character is found where there is inner harmony, everything fitting together nicely, and nothing causing discord. That doesn't mean the absence of problems, nor the non-existence of some tensions. It means, rather, that there is no element there that doesn't belong with the rest. No character is beautiful where everything is in order except for the presence of dishonesty. Dishonesty mars all the rest, clashing violently with it like a clownish necklace of frankfurters on a queen's coronation gown. Wherever any single sin looms large in the life of an otherwise splendid person we have the sensation of being confronted with ugliness. Beauty has been spoiled. But where we find virtues harmoniously existing together in a life, all present and each in proportion to the others, there we have beautiful character. Beauty is a by-product of inner order and harmony.

Ralph Waldo Emerson, a student of human nature, made an observation in his essay, "Conduct of Life," that applies the meaning of beauty to human nature: "There is no beautifier of complexion, or form, or behavior, like the wish to scatter joy and not pain around us." As a beauty aid, apply a little of that idea to your soul three times daily, and rub vigorously.

*Eleven*

# BEAUTY EXPRESSED IN ACTION

MOST WILD BIRDS find the sound of trickling water nearly irresistible. Water that is alive, moving, and making small, labial sounds, will entice birds as a flame attracts moths on a summer's night. Many a gardener takes advantage of the affection birds have for running water by building a small pool in his garden and an artificial waterfall or a small jet fountain to provide a sparkle of lively action and a tinkle of liquid sound.

Much of the grace found in nature is expressed in movement, the skipping of a brook over stones, the sway of birches in the wind, the slow beat of a sea gull's wings, the smooth glide of a hawk upon an upswept current of air, the flowing, elegant ease of a deer bounding over low brush and logs, the lazy lap of waves upon a lake shore – all these witness to the beauty of motion in nature.

Human nature needs quietness and leisurely contemplation if it is to produce its best effect – just as Leonardo Da Vinci sometimes stood for hours before his unfinished painting, "The Last Supper," before making a brush stroke on the canvas. Still, there could be no paintings without brush strokes, and no great living without great deeds. Action is necessary, and nothing in human experience is more attractive and winsome than a noble thought or emotion in the process of becoming a deed.

One day a lad carrying a basket of eggs down the street tripped on a curbstone and sprawled headlong on the pavement. The eggs were smashed. A crowd of sympathizers gathered around the sobbing youngster. One dear old lady cried, "Dear me, what a pity!" A man exclaimed, "Poor little fellow; I hope his dad doesn't give him a trimming." One matronly looking woman said tenderly, "There, there. Now don't cry." Then a man stepped out from the crowd and declared, "I care fifty cents' worth." Another announced, "I care a quarter's worth." In a few moments the boy had

enough money for another basket of eggs, because some people translated sympathy into action.

One of the most beautiful sights in the world is graceful movement, especially when good feeling is being expressed in a good deed.

*Twelve*

# SOME INCARNATIONS I HAVE KNOWN

THE WORD "incarnation" refers to a theological idea dear to Christians everywhere, the embodiment of God in human flesh in the person of Christ. The word comes from the Latin, meaning "in flesh." But long before there was a doctrine of incarnation, the early Christians had experiences with Jesus that made such a teaching inevitable. He made God seem near, believable, and in some measure understandable. He showed to them in what He said, in what He did, and in what He was, something of what God is like. They believed that if they could grasp what Jesus would do in any situation they would then know what God would have them do in the same circumstances, because He so perfectly embodied the will of God. God seemed far away. Jesus was near. God was unseen. Jesus was visible, audible, touchable. God seemed abstract. Jesus was God in a carpenter's apron, wielding a mallet and chisel, or God in friendship and conversation, God with helping hands.

The doctrine of the incarnation is an attempt to put into words something that most of us feel is true about life's best and worst. The good and the evil alike are constantly seeking embodiment.

It is nearly impossible to think of beauty in the abstract. It is far easier and more natural to think of something in particular that is beautiful – a timid doe with her month-old fawn appearing at our brook's edge, or the amber waters of a stream dancing and singing around stones and logs, or the sound of an exuberant song sparrow's bubbling music. Try to hold the idea of beauty in your mind for a moment. Abstract it from every form, sound, odor, and feeling, if you can. Try to keep this abstraction detached from all your experiences with lovely things. There now, see how impossible it is to maintain such an abstraction for long? The idea of beauty persists in becoming clothed in some experi-

ence with sunsets or stars, animals or persons, sights or sounds. Beauty demands embodiment.

Evil, as well as good, detests abstractions and constantly seeks some concrete expression. It pushes itself into the experience of man in the form of needless suffering, or in a particular crime or an injustice, in floods, tornadoes and droughts, in scatter-brained driving on the highways, in slums and abject poverty. Evil employs the stratagem of getting itself mixed up in homes, in politics, in clubs, and even in churches, where it can be expressed in irritability or underhandedness, jealousy and bigotry, or in any of a multitude of slightly disguised forms. Evil takes on flesh and reveals itself in a Hitler or Stalin, a John Dillinger or Al Capone, in a gossiper, a chronic hater, or a belittler. If evil would only remain formless, disembodied, how innocuous it would be!

This is the glory of the incarnation of God – it need not be confined to the birth of Christ. It can happen again and again. Never again will it occur just as it did in Bethlehem, for there could be only one of Him, but to the measure of our smaller capacity God still invests Himself in something tangible and touchable.

His love of beauty I have seen in the cobalt-colored waters of an inland lake, in the flash of a whitetail deer streaking through a forest glade, and in the limpid lavender of a wild violet's face.

His truth I have seen framed by a child's guileless, bold tongue and lips, in a child who "knows no better" than to speak his mind, and in the candor of a friend who would rather speak the plain fact that hurts than the flattery that soothes.

His goodness I have observed in an old man who, though much abused and maligned, refused to hate, and forgave. I have seen it in the life of one whose response to being hurt was to love.

His greatness I have seen in the bigness of some people I know whose helpful hands know neither race nor class nor creed but whose concern for all is so inclusive that their arms are stretched toward any who will turn to them.

These are some incarnations I have known. God still seeks to clothe Himself in flesh. Does He in ours?

*Thirteen*

# ON KEEPING YOUR BALANCE

To the question: "How does a fish swim?" most people would answer, "With its fins, of course." But this is one of the many "of courses," the natural assumptions about Nature's children, that are not so. Most fishes do not swim with their fins at all.

Take our Lake Charlevoix yellow perch, for example. They, like their bass and sunfish and pike cousins, swim with their tails rather than their fins. The appendages we know as "fins" – the dorsal fin lying on the ridge of the back, the pectoral fins that lie just back of the gills, the pelvic and anal fins that lie along the abdomen – are all used by perch for steering and stabilizing the fish, and most of all for maintaining balance. Actual swimming is done with the tail, which whips from side to side in a sculling motion, propelling the fish forward.

Even a slight knowledge of the anatomy of the earth's children is enough to convince the observer that the Creator has given much attention to providing His creatures with equipment for maintaining their balance. Fins on perch, long bushy tails on fox squirrels, the heavy stout tails of kangaroos, the tails of the king crab, the semi-circular canals in the inner ear of such mammals as man – all serve the purpose of helping the creature to maintain its balance.

But balance in nature is far more than a matter of creatures possessing special equipment for remaining upright. Balance is a fundamental principle integral with nature and necessary to life as we know it on this planet. We see the essential nature of balance illustrated in the proportions of birds to insects and small mammals on a certain acreage of land. Songbirds feed upon insects and weed-seeds. Hawks and owls devour large numbers of meadow mice and white-footed mice, which consume remarkable amounts of grain. If stray, half-wild cats, or boys with air rifles kill off the songbirds, the insects and weeds thrive and become serious threats

to the farmers. If boys and men shoot down every hawk and owl they see, the grain-hungry mice multiply prodigiously. Farmers suffer when such a balance is upset. The grasses of pasture would soon be gone if birds did not thin out the grubs, and trees in the forests would soon disappear if nuthatches, chickadees, and their winged cousins did not wage perpetual war on all manner of injurious insects.

Whenever man upsets nature's balance, he brings woe upon himself. Rats were brought by ship to Jamaica and, having nearly no natural enemies, soon multiplied to the proportions of a plague. The rat-eating mongoose was then imported to cope with the rats. In a short time the weasel-like mongoose had accomplished its mission, having cleaned up all the imported rats and the Jamaican cane rats. Then it began seeking other prey and found it. Jamaican poultry and songbirds and insect-eating lizards were the substitutes. They fell before the mongoose in great hordes. Then insects, which songbirds, poultry, and lizards had held in check, infested the land, and it all started when man foolishly or negligently brought a few Old World rats to Jamaica.

Tragic consequences in human life follow upsetting nature's balances. Our organic life is delicately balanced and easily disturbed and ended. If our temperature goes a few degrees above 98.6 degrees we can die of the fever, and if it goes a bit below normal the end result is the same. A little too much thyroxin or too little is enough to make invalids of us or to terminate our stay here. If a person eats too much food or too little, he suffers. If he exercises too hard or too little, his body is distressed. Too little rest or too much is harmful. Disease is usually a loss of balance in some part of the body or in all of it. And it is when the breaking-down processes get too far ahead of the building-up processes that death ensues.

Emotional balance, too, is needed. Too little or too much emotion are signs of mental disturbance. Total inhibition of all of one's feelings or wild expression of all one's urges will be equally detrimental to one's mental health and to one's usefulness.

One of the most pitiable sights on the face of the earth is

lopsided virtue. The scribes and Pharisees of Jesus' time were affected with it. They cherished the past, which is good and commendable, but they were blind to new insights that the present day offered them. They were aware of what God had said to Moses but deaf to what God was saying to them in their own time. They were excited about enforcing the minute, fine points of the law, but they often missed the grand and sweeping spirit of their religion. That sort of lopsidedness has not disappeared from religious circles. It is a sign of a diseased spirit. The person who abides by all the rules of religion and still is ungracious and spiritually unattractive is unbalanced. The ultra-pious, who can find a Scripture text to support every prejudice but who cannot read in current events and in the lives of their contemporaries, in nature and in their own life-adventures, what God is saying to them now, are only half alive.

One is equally wrong in having an arrogant sense of his own self-importance or in groveling in whining inferiority. Both the person who is so rigid that he can never change his opinion and the one who is constantly changing his mind are mentally unhealthy. Some people are so indifferent to others' needs that they will do nothing for others unless they are sure of reward. Others are so soft-hearted that they are foolishly victimized by their husbands, wives, children, and acquaintances and help make of them self-seeking ingrates, and both are miserable and contribute to the spiritual hardship of those near them.

If we are to be at our best, we need to claim for ourselves some of the balance God has built into nature. Here are some balances we can profitably seek:

(1) A balance between getting and giving.

(2) A balance between withdrawing into the shelter of our faith and going out into the world to expose our faith.

(3) A balance between destroying evil and building the good.

(4) A balance between acquiring more knowledge on how to handle life and applying what knowledge we already have.

(5) A balanced emphasis between life's means and its ends,

between the techniques of living and the purpose for which we live.

(6) A balance between life's restraints and its freedoms, having enough but not too much of each.

(7) A balance between fretful discontent and contented lethargy.

(8) A balance between hard work and satisfying rest.

(9) A balance between seeking privileges and assuming responsibilities.

(10) A balance between life's tough outward circumstances and rich and dependable inner resources.

Many a patient in a hospital, imprisoned in casts and swathed in bandages, has explained his fall by saying: "I just lost my balance." Loss of balance explains many a moral and spiritual tragedy, too.

There is an old benediction which says, "Now unto him that is able to keep you from falling, and to present you faultless before the presence of his glory with exceeding joy, to the only wise God our Saviour, be glory and majesty, dominion and power, both now and ever. Amen." He "that is able to keep you from falling" – how does He do it? Usually by showing us, in the life of the Supreme Example, how a man keeps his balance.

*Fourteen*

# WHEN THE DROUGHTS COME

THE HEARTLIKE tracks are more plentiful by the brook, now that summer's heat is at its highest. Among the rocks and roots, the ferns and grasses that bind the brook's banks to keep them from unraveling, we find an intermingling of prints big and small. In the winter some are there. In spring and fall they are plentiful. But upon a summer's morning the brookside near certain favorite deer haunts is carpeted with a dense all-over pattern of whitetail tracks.

In the deep dark of the night, while the forest leaves whisper in their sleep, matronly does creep from cedar thickets, with dappled fawns mincing along behind, and drink long and deeply of the frosty, tasty brook waters. They drink from a deep inner longing to quench the fiery thirst of millions of deer tissues that urgently call for moisture. For most of the year deer have no such thirst and drink but occasionally. The succulent herbaceous plants and the moist weeds and grasses upon which they forage in the spring provide needed moisture. Fall rains and long-lasting dews wetting the whitetails' favorite foods make much drinking unnecessary in the autumn. Less water is lost from the deer through perspiration and evaporation in the cold of winter, and some moisture is ingested when particles of snow are eaten along with winter foods. But the whitetails' summer foods are often as dry as shredded-wheat biscuit, and the loss of moisture in their bodies is appalling. When summer droughts come, deer drink the most. They must, or perish.

When life is driest, we need to use the simple wisdom of the deer. We are often tempted to do otherwise. When testings come, disappointments assail us, or a withering crisis, like a summer's sizzling sun, glares down upon us, we withdraw the farthest from life's refreshing streams. We worry more, we fret more. We retreat from people and mope in self-pity. The measures we take, far from bracing and renewing our strength, exhaust and weaken us.

When the droughts come and we are dried out and athirst, we might best, like the deer, steal away to sources of refreshment.

Worship will help, because it fixes our minds upon enduring values, the imperishables, the eternal things and the Eternal One. Beside these our low moods seem almost insignificant.

Fellowship with good people will help, too. As the merging of two brooks will make a stream larger than either of them, the confluence of two good minds will make for a strength greater than one can have alone.

Help someone else. It is easier to carry two pieces of heavy luggage, one in each hand, than it is to carry only one big piece. One makes you lopsided, and tires you rapidly. Two pieces balance each other. So another's burden, added to your own, will rest you, refresh you. Try it and see.

When the droughts come, instead of exhausting yourself with fretfulness and worry, seek streams of strength and renewal.

*Fifteen*

# SIZE AND QUALITY

A PFRSON does not need to observe the realm of plant life for long before he will notice two things. He will be awed by the diversity in form and size among members of the plant kingdom, and he will see that size and quality may be almost wholly unrelated.

Side by side near our brook grow towering trees and short shrubs of flowering raspberries. A large maple, an ash, or a spruce will outweigh a lowly raspberry shrub many thousands of times, and to the calculating eye of a lumberman a tree's worth is far greater than that of a shrub, even though the latter is spangled with a glory of snowy white and pink flowers. But Nature's scheme of values is different, and in the plan of things the raspberry will be wholly as important as the trees that shade it. Maples, ash, and spruce provide nesting sites for birds, shade for the stream and shadow-loving wild flowers, food for all manner of insect-eating songbirds and fuel for our fireplace. But the raspberry will feed ruffed grouse and chickadee, bluejay, kingbird, phoebe and robin, song sparrow, white-throated sparrow, scarlet tanager and wood thrush, red fox and varying hare, cottontail rabbit and ring-tailed raccoon, squirrel and chipmunk, white-footed mouse, and white-tailed deer. Wild raspberries provide a summer banquet for the wild creatures on our acres. They are illustrations of nature's perpetual lesson that size and usefulness bear no necessary relationship to each other.

The smallest flowering plant in this country is a duckweed, or wolffia, a tiny speck of floating greenness, a mere one twenty-fifth of an inch in diameter, often found in quiet ponds and streams. At the other extreme is a gigantic denizen of the dense forest of the Sierra Nevada mountains, the General Sherman tree, one of the sequoia trees. Its trunk is 36 feet in diameter and 272 feet high, and its weight is estimated at over a thousand tons. Yet in the economy of nature the giant sequoia and the minute duckweed each

have a place of equal importance. The sequoia cannot be the food of multitudes of ducks and vast throngs of fishes. The duckweed can be and is. Nor can houses be built of duckweed, while they are built from sequoias. In nature the littlest and biggest things alike are parts of a wondrous plan, and size and importance may be wholly unrelated.

What is true of plants is so of men. Big men are not necessarily big souls, nor are small men of necessity spiritual pigmies. Quality of life and size of body have little to do with each other, and little heads may produce great thoughts. During the past one hundred years the United States has had no President whom history has proven wiser or greater than Abraham Lincoln. During the bleak days of the Civil War Lincoln was nearly the only one in Washington to keep his head. Yet that head was singularly small for so large a man as Lincoln was. Abraham Lincoln wore a seven and one-eighth size hat, and no President since his time has worn a hat so small, with the exception of Calvin Coolidge. Garfield's hat was a big one – size seven and three-fourths. Grant, Taft, and Franklin Roosevelt wore large hats – size seven and five-eighths. Cleveland's and Benjamin Harrison's hats were seven and one-half. Seven and three-eighths was the size of Theodore Roosevelt's hat. So was Warren Harding's. Apparently there is no relationship between size of head and quality of mind.

This lesson learned from nature needs to be generously applied to other realms, for we Americans are so easily overwhelmed by size. We are like the disciples of Jesus who walked through the streets of Jerusalem with the Master one day and came to the temple. It was a huge building – much bigger than they were accustomed to seeing in their native Galilee, and they exclaimed, "Look, Teacher, what a size these stones and buildings are!" But Jesus remained unimpressed by size and bulk. He never was over-awed by the size of anything – stones, buildings, crowds, purses. He gave as careful attention to one listener at His feet as He did to a crowd of five thousand. He showered as much affection on little children as He did upon adults. Jesus was unmoved by mere bigness. Not size, but quality impressed Him.

What counts everlastingly is not the bigness of our churches, the size of the crowds an event may attract, the number of cubic feet of space in our houses, the pile of books we have read, the length of our cars, or the size of our bank accounts. The only bigness that counts in first-century Palestine or twentieth-century America is bigness of soul.

*Sixteen*

# A WORLD OF OPPOSITES

THE PEOPLE I pity when summer comes are those who have missed winter in the North. They see what the rest of us see but without fully savoring it, just as victims of a heavy cold can eat a banquet meal but cannot taste delicate shades of flavoring.

Purple finches singing from our apple boughs mean more to those who have known the silence of winter to be broken only by an occasional chickadee's call. Apple blossoms and developing fruit seem more lively, vital, and rich with meaning if you have seen the same boughs as somber as death, weighed down by snow and sleet. Grass looks greener when one remembers the pale whiteness of the land only a few months ago.

The natural world is full of sharp contrasts, winter and summer, stiff winds and dead calm, high hills and deep valleys, quiet ponds and turbulent streams, stygian darkness and brilliant lights, sunsets and dawns. The enjoyment of Nature is found in seeing her in all her moods.

Life, too, is crammed full of opposites, and living a full life involves a recognition and appreciation of the contrasts.

We must occasionally behold ugliness if we are to appreciate beauty.

There can be no such thing as "high" unless there is also a "low."

Without an East there could be no West, without a North, no South.

We must experience noise if we are to savor the luxury of silence.

We find the shade most genial when we have spent hours sweating under the hot sun.

We must know hard work if we are to feel the pleasure of rest.

Water is most delicious and refreshing when thirst is the greatest.

We must have a sense of failure if we are to know the relief of forgiveness.

Those who have never known harsh disappointment or deep grief can hardly attain a height of joy.

Unless some crisis has brought you to the brink of death and shocked you with awareness of the brevity and delicacy of life, you can hardly appreciate the value of a year, or a month, or a day, of living.

Life's contrasts do two things for me. The awareness of life's opposites makes me impatient with the namby-pamby attitude that "it doesn't matter what you believe, as long as you believe something!" It does matter. It matters consummately. This is a world of opposing values where one must be taking sides constantly, and it matters what side you take. Liking the good in life involves disliking the bad, and loving the highest means detesting the mediocre. The gardener who loves flowers must also hate weeds.

Moreover, a consciousness of life's opposites makes me grateful for the undesirable and uncomfortable experiences that come my way, because I know that they heighten my enjoyment of the good.

*Seventeen*

# YOUR CHIEF COMPETITOR

ONE REASON I enjoy our wild animal brethren is because they are so innocent of a common human fault – our insane pride in competitiveness.

That fawn born late last May and hidden and nursed on our wild acres is growing at a rate all his own, not caring whether he is smaller or bigger than other fawns that saw the light of day in his natal month. (If he eats well he may attain the weight of 75 to 100 pounds by the time he is six months old, gaining one-third pound per day or more.) He is untainted by any arrogance at having more white spots on his heaving sides than do other fawns living in the same woods and pastures. Regardless of what other fawns may do, when the time comes to lose his spots, he will lose them, probably late in September. He may now run faster than his neighbors, or slower, but his greater speed will not engender conceit, nor would loss in a race across a sunlit meadow trouble his sleep. A fawn, like his animal cousins and bird neighbors, is quite content to live and grow at his own rate and in his own way, without making disdainful or discouraging comparisons. I like that about animals.

We humans are born into a society that teaches us to strive to be first among our fellows, with the result that our happiness depends less upon our real achievements in life than it does upon making favorable comparisons between ourselves and others. Customarily our joys do not depend upon our doing a good job, or even an excellent one, but upon beating our nearest competitor. Our chief regrets are not that we have failed to meet a high standard of performance, but that we have lost out to a rival. Ordinarily we could be fairly well satisfied with even a mediocre record as long as we surpassed all our competitors. This is equally true of our most personal relations with our acquaintances and with the relationships among the world's great nations.

Sometimes our competitiveness is expressed in a childish craving for predominance. A Polish family which had lived next door moved away, and a lonely little American girl was in tears. Her mother asked her the reason for her crying, and the youngster explained that she was sad because the Polish family had left. This astonished the mother. "I didn't realize you loved them so much," she said.

"Oh, it isn't that," the little girl confessed; "but now that they have moved there is nobody that I can feel better than!"

For some of us that is one of life's essentials, to have someone near toward whom we can feel superior.

Sometimes competitiveness goes to such lengths that it is neurotic. Then a person measures himself against others in every situation — even in circumstances that do not warrant competition. It may be natural enough for two beauty contestants to question which is the more beautiful, or for two singers to ask themselves which has the better voice, or for two political contestants to question which is the more popular. But the person whose competitiveness has gotten out of hand applies such questions without discrimination — always, everywhere, and under all circumstances making comparisons between self and others, asking who is more beautiful, who has the better voice, or who is more popular. He wants to be ahead of everyone and is miserable if he is not. If the question is one of popularity, he measures his own acceptance by the public against that of everyone, secretly wondering,

"Am I more popular than he?" when he faces the butcher, the baker, and the candlestick maker, as well as his political opponent.

So with intelligence. The person plagued with neurotic competitiveness must be ahead of everyone or he is uncomfortable. If someone in his group can out-talk him, being better informed or wittier, he is inwardly disgraced. As a result he can hardly savor any fellowship and be thoroughly satisfied by it, unless he comes out on top in what he considers as the race for approval and respect. Nor can he give his complete and dedicated attention to any cause because his first loyalty is to himself, and his first aim is conquest over other minds rather than the advancement of a great purpose.

The competitor makes himself wretched in another way. Not only must he be better than anyone else at one point, such as in popularity or intelligence, but often he seeks to be best in everything. Thus he stretches toward an impossible goal. His excessive ambition draws him in dozens of directions at once and, since he cannot possibly be the best in everything, makes him feel defeated in many of the projects he attempts. He cannot enjoy painting as a hobby, because his pictures must be better than anyone else's. He can hardly converse comfortably, because he must be the best conversationalist in the group, and if his circle of friends (competitors, to him) turn to playing croquet, he must win or suffer abject inner defeat. Since no one can be best at everything, the neurotic competitor will always be inwardly distressed, no matter how well he can "grin and bear it" outwardly.

Even the competitor's successes are usually bound to be disappointing to him. There is still someone, somewhere up ahead of him. That spoils everything. If he sings, there is someone in the world who can outsing him. If he paints, somewhere on earth there is someone who can paint better. If he speaks in public and does well, soon along comes someone who is a better orator. No matter how fast he runs, some day his record will be broken. Even his greatest successes are dimmed by the haunting awareness that someone, somewhere, is better, or someday will be better.

Moreover, the unfettered ambition of wild competitiveness

makes a person dangerously aggressive. His longing to be best carries with it an implicit hostility that determines that no one else shall be quite capable, quite intelligent, quite successful. If he is to reach the mark, everyone else must fall short of it. So he secretly delights in another's defeat. He is inwardly pleased at another's faults. And if the faults are not apparent he must imagine them and talk about them. If his pride is in intelligence, another person's mistakes are the result of being "stupid." If his pride is in popularity, another's disgrace "serves him right for being such a social climber." Others must be cut down to size, which means below his own level.

Is there a sensible antidote to our foolish, overgrown competitiveness? There is. One kind of contest is noble and justifiable – regard yourself as your chief competitor. Outplay yourself. Improve on your own record. Regard the person you were yesterday as the one you must beat today. There is adventure in that, and satisfaction, too.

What a difference it would make in our businesses if every businessman and business organization did not try to "cut the other fellow's throat" but constantly improved his own products and his services! Every product on the markets of the world can be made more cheaply and sold for less – if all we want is cheapness. Every craft can be exercised more carelessly and shoddily for less money, if cost-competition among the crafts and trades is most desirable. But we need something in our business world besides low prices. We need pride in workmanship, delight in high quality, and satisfaction in rendering an improved service, and to achieve these things we must develop in business the kind of

competition that counts most – the intense desire to outstrip yesterday.

We need such a purpose in international life, too – not to excel the record of another nation, but to become daily a better America, a better member of the family of nations, and a better symbol and example of freedom and hope. It is not enough to get ahead or to stay ahead of the Russians. We must get ahead of the America we are at any given moment of history.

In personal life such competition means a prolonged childhood of the spirit, perpetual growth. It means being a bit bigger and wiser today than you were yesterday. In all the contests that matter most, you are your chief competitor.

*Eighteen*

# ON SEEING WHAT IS THERE

THE BEST FISHERMAN is not one who merely knows how to play a fly rod or casting rod so as to make a lure look lifelike and tantalizingly desirable to his prey. The sportsman who consistently out-fishes his companions and returns home with his limit while his friends have near-empty creels, is one who recognizes a good fishing spot when he sees it.

The bluegill enthusiast will know that the likeliest place for his choicest pan fish is a protected cove, where wind does not ruffle the water. He will seek out well-sheltered places where lily pads cast a cooling shadow or where other water-plants grow high from the lake bottom and provide hiding among their leaves. And he will be aware that, try as he might, he will catch no bluegills from cold, swiftly flowing shallow streams. That is good trout territory, but not for bluegills.

But the experienced trout fisherman will not seek brook trout in bluegill water, either. The ardent brookie fan knows that his intended victim will most likely be found in a cool stream that affords much concealment and in a spot that permits the trout to examine a current for floating food. Yet there must be a nearby cushion of more slowly moving water which allows the fish to stay in one place without undue expenditure of effort. The backwater of a large pool in a stream may be ideal. Or a trout may lie in the protecting shadow of a large mid-stream boulder and watch for passing food. Under-water stump roots, overhanging branches, undercut banks, sunken logs and places where spring-fed streamlets enter a larger sweep of water – all of these signify the possible presence of trout.

When searching for delicately flavored walleyed pike in the springtime, the knowing angler will fish in shallow water over sand bars, along rocky reefs, in the rapids of tumbling rivers and over the bottoms of dark bays. But during the heat of summer the fisherman will try the cool depths of deep water during the days and the edges of weed beds, reefs and sand bars at night. The walleye, like every other kind of fish, has its favorite habitat, and the sportsman who, day after day, makes the biggest and best catches is one who can tell by a few outward signs what must lie underneath the surface awaiting his lure.

So it is with our daily living. Some people are making big catches of enjoyment, happiness, spiritual satisfaction, and appreciation because they can read signs and imagine what is below the surface. Others see the same signs but do not properly interpret them as pointing to the hidden presence of something significant. They don't understand what they mean. They can't take a hint, and so their creels remain empty.

This is especially true of the opportunities life affords us. Two people will see the same thing or be confronted with the same circumstances, and one will moan about how cruelly life has treated him, while the other feels excited by the challenge of a problem to be mastered.

Some years ago two shoe salesmen, one American and the other British, embarked on the same boat to West Africa. Upon landing they looked around and were impressed by the fact that all the natives were barefoot. The Britisher, discouraged, cabled his home office: "Poor territory. Nobody here wears shoes. Will return home by next ship."

The American rushed to the cable office and fired off this message to his chief: "Market wide open. Nobody here wearing shoes. Send one million pairs on consignment." The conditions were the same for both men, but only the one recognized an opportunity when he saw it. Some see discouragement in every opportunity. Others see opportunity in every discouragement.

Everyone sooner or later faces a crisis in his life. When it comes, some people panic and others prove heroic. The difference between these two reactions is due to one's interpretation of what a crisis is. The Chinese word for "crisis" is made up of two characters, "way" meaning "danger" and "gee" meaning opportunity. In the Chinese language a crisis is a dangerous opportunity. In any man's language the character of a crisis depends upon what he sees in the experience, final disaster or an occasion for building character and a better way of life.

The power to recognize good "fishing grounds" applies to our dealings with people, too. We are not so apt to make bad people good as we are to recognize and encourage the latent good that lies beneath the surface of commonplace-appearing lives. No king ever made a man a knight. The best a king could do was to recognize the knighthood already present in a man. As Phillips Brooks once put it: "The king lays a sword on a man's shoulder and calls him a knight; but he was a knight before he was knighted or he would not have received the title. It was the heroic endurance, the death-defying courage, the skill and coolness with which he achieved his notable deeds that made him a knight. He was in himself royal and noble and the king said to all men, I see it, when he laid his sword on his shoulder."

No church can make a saint. Not all of Christendom together could make a saint of a man who had not really been one. The best the Church can do is to cultivate and then recognize the God-instilled saintliness in a person and call it to the attention of the world. Saint Augustine and Saint Francis of Assisi are not saints because the Church says they are, but the Church simply recognized the sainthood of those men and called the world's attention to the holiness that was there long before the Church discovered it.

The best men and women who ever walked our earth were at the same time ridiculed by some and revered by others. Their scoffers and followers all saw the same persons, but some construed what they saw as signs of stupidity, or insanity, or unorthodoxy, or evil intent, while others interpreted what they observed as signs of greatness. Then the long years rolled by and the greatest and best are sanctioned by history. But history does not make men great. It merely recognizes the greatness that was there all along.

Whether we are dealing with discouragement, a sudden crisis, or with greatness passing by, if we are to come to the end of life's brief day with a creel full of enduring satisfactions we must learn to read the signs of value, so that in our circumstances and in our fellow-men we may be aware of the good that is there.

*Nineteen*

# ON BEING ALIVE

"LIFE" IS A WORD that occurs frequently in our vocabulary without our knowing exactly what it means. In a vague way we understand what "life" is, but try to define it specifically without consulting a dictionary. What is alive and what is not?

The raccoon that snatches his lunch of crayfish or mussels from our woodland stream is alive. So is the bunchberry that blooms on the brook bank in summer. So are the trees that shade the laughing waters. But the rocks that dimple the stream's surface are not alive. Nor is the water itself. Ground pine is alive, but the soil from which it grows is not. But what are the differences between the living and non-living things of a woodland?

For one thing, it is clear that living things must have food, and they seek it. Food-seeking seems to be the chief preoccupation of most living things, whether it be a raccoon fishing in a stream, a deer browsing on maple shoots, a fox prowling for deer-mice, a dragonfly hunting mosquitoes, or a wild plant searching in the soil for chemicals and moisture and trapping sunlight for starch-making. All living things seek food for staying alive. A rock has no hunger nor does a raindrop or a stretch of flowing water.

Moreover, living things repair their worn and injured parts by new growth. Non-living things do not. As a raccoon's hair or a mink's whiskers, or a whitetail buck's antlers are shed, new ones are grown to replace them. As a plant's leaves drop off, new leaves are grown to take their place. Some of the food these living things digest is used in making these necessary repairs. Growth of new cells and tissues is typical of living things.

Not so with the non-living. As the swift waters of a stream jostle the rocks against each other and they are worn, they do not replace their lost mass with new growth. As the naturalist's shoe soles wear from walking on forest floor and

-KOHN-

stony beach, they do not grow new leather. A shoemaker may repair them, but they cannot grow the material to repair themselves. The power of growth is peculiar to living things.

Living things give birth to young. Non-living things do not. Plants have seeds or offshoots. Human mothers cuddle reproductions of themselves. But big boats do not give birth to little skiffs, nor do bicycles have tricycles.

There are other differences between organic and inorganic things, but the fundamental contrasts are in the power to hunger and feed, the power to digest food and translate it into growth, and the power to reproduce.

The life of the spirit is much like that of the flesh in these three respects. A person who is fully alive is one who has appetite, who feeds upon and digests the good in the world about him and translates it into growth of spirit. And the alive person is one who leaves a generation of goodness behind him when he passes from this life. He reproduces goodness.

Now, how alive are you? Do you have a healthy appetite, a hungry mind? What do you crave to know?

The perverseness of bodily appetite is almost unimaginable, children being known to eat dirt, polish, scraped paint from walls and furniture, hair, wool and cotton, paper, plaster, ashes, buttons and strings, soap, pebbles, bugs, and worms. But stranger still is the waywardness of mental appetite in human beings. One of the wonders of human nature is the bizarre character of the things we hunger for and crave to know or want to possess. When John Dillinger, the notorious outlaw of the 1930's, was shot in Chicago, one reporter witnessed the sight of little children dipping their handkerchiefs in the bandit's blood which was spilled on the pavement. One man offered a thousand dollars for the outlaw's shirt, and another a thousand dollars for his shoes. It is reported that when the coroner gave Dillinger's aged father the $7.70 that had been in the bandit's pocket, he said, "Now, don't spend any of this money. Morbid-minded America will pay you a fortune for it."

Contrast with such morbidity the healthy-minded appetite of which Jesus spoke. The Master one time said, "Blessed are they that hunger and thirst after righteousness, for they shall be filled." Well, for what do you hunger and thirst? After the right things, the highest?

What are you curious about?

What news do you enjoy hearing about your acquaintances – their blunders and failures, or their successes and triumphs?

What do you look for in the newspapers? What interests you most in magazines and books – scandal, gossip, or beauty and goodness?

How is your appetite?

Another question – how is your digestion? All living things take material from outside of their beings, absorb it into their bodies and transform this matter chemically into energy and movement and growth. A Hidden Brook raccoon reaches into the stream for small aquatic animals, rinses them off, chucks them into his mouth and they are broken up by his digestive system, and the nutriments are distributed by his blood system to build new raccoon body cells. The low-growing bunchberry sends its roots into the damp earth and uses the richness it finds there for building greenish-white flower clusters, shiny green leaves, and bright red globular berries. All living things at Hidden Brook and elsewhere on the broad earth are assimilators of good they find around them.

How alive are you? Can you take from your environment the good that is there and absorb it into your way of life? Can you send the taproots of your thinking down into a situation and assimilate the nutritional elements that are there? One person can look at the glorious stripes of color that comprise a sunset and murmur, "That reminds me, wife, let's have bacon for breakfast tomorrow." Another beholding the same grandeur exclaims, "The heavens declare the glory of God and the firmament showeth His handiwork!" The one gets no good out of the glory spread before him; he is but reminded of one more thing he wants. The other makes awe, wonder, and reverence out of what his mind absorbs.

One visitor to an European art museum grumbled about the old masterpieces the guide was showing him. "What is all the fuss about?" he muttered. "I can't see anything in

those old paintings that deserves so much praise and such an expensive showing." The guide took all he could and then turned on the unappreciative complainer. "Listen, Mister," he exclaimed, "these pictures are no longer on trial. You are!"

The best things in life – great paintings, fine literature, good music, profound religion, marriage, the home – are no longer on trial. We are. What good do you absorb from them and use in building stronger character, bigger mind, and greater soul? How is your digestion?

Are you still changing and growing? All living things change or perish. Whenever a person dies it is because some part of the body that is worn or injured does not grow new tissues in time to replace the old. In a plant or animal, in a ground pine, a raccoon, or growing boy, as organs wear out, tissue by tissue they are rapidly repaired through rest and nutrition. But when one gets far enough in arrears through lack of rest or nutrition, or accident or disease, death is the certain result. Natural death occurs whenever new growth does not repair injured or worn cells.

The life of the spirit is much like that of the flesh. We must keep on growing or die. Life constantly wears on our courage. It wearies our love. It exhausts our patience. It tires our spirit of helpfulness. Unless there is inspiration to match our expenditures we waste away. How about it? Are you growing new courage, love, patience, helpfulness? Are you becoming stronger? Are you a bigger and better person than you were last year, last month, and yesterday?

And lastly, another striking difference between living and non-living things is in the power to reproduce themselves. After it has finished flowering, the bunchberry plant will develop seeds in its little red berry, and when these seeds are carried away by bird or beast and fall upon favorable ground new bunchberry plants will sprout and grow. The maple will spill winged seeds upon the winds and some distant day young maples will sway to the tune of Hidden Brook breezes. The raccoon will father little coonlets.

But the skillet at Hideaway House will never bear baby frying pans, nor will our house give birth to little cottages, nor our chairs have litters of little stools. The power to reproduce themselves belongs to living things alone.

Just as every living thing on earth is the reproduction of some other thing that lived before it, so every inspired person is the product of an inspirer. Every good life has issued from some other person who lived splendidly. Every believer in God has come to Him through some other believer. Good living things reproduce themselves. It is in this way that goodness is maintained upon the earth.

How alive are you? Are the good things in your life being reproduced in the lives of others so that they will be here long after you are gone? Are you passing on to future generations the best that is in you?

One old saint was once heard to pray, "Lord, keep me alive as long as I live." While existing here, are you showing signs of being alive?

*Twenty*

# ONE WAY TO FIND REST

SLEEP IS ONE of life's essentials for all the highly developed animals. The eminent British biologist, J. Arthur Thomson, has declared that animals accustomed to sleep will die in a few days if deprived of it. It has been demonstrated experimentally that if some animals are robbed of sleep they will die much sooner than if denied food.

Both clinical data and everyday observation show that adequate sleep is important to human beings. It removes evidences of fatigue, freshens the sleeper, and permits recovery from the strain of activity. But many a person finds slumber elusive. Insomnia can have many causes, such as physical pain, or tensions aroused by guilt or ego-wounding memories, worries and fears, and concern with one's prestige. Some insomnia can be treated medically and other kinds by penitence with its resulting sense of forgiveness, by spiritual cleansing from all hatreds and resentments, or by the development of new and simple habits, such as retiring at the same time every night, taking warm, relaxing baths and the conscious avoidance of excitement prior to going to bed.

Often, however, sleeplessness stems from faithlessness. Some people cannot rest because they will not leave themselves and the world in God's hands. They feel that their own destiny and an improved world situation depend upon their being awake and constantly on the job. They are like a minor executive who never dares to take a vacation from his office for fear the company will not survive his absence. He does not have faith in the chief executive's capacity to carry on. The creedal statement, "I believe in God," means more than acknowledging His existence. It implies trust. To trust God means to believe He is watchful and working for our own good and the world's welfare while we rest, and that the general management of the universe is in good hands.

William Beebe, the naturalist, has told of visits he made to the home of Theodore Roosevelt, whose love for nature was well known. Often, after an evening's talk at Roosevelt's Sagamore Hill home, the two men would leave the house, walk over the great, spreading lawn, and look up into the night sky. They would vie with each other to see who could first identify the pale bit of light-mist near the upper left-hand corner of the Great Square of Pegasus, and then either Roosevelt or Beebe would recite:

"That is the Spiral Galaxy of Andromeda. It is as large as our Milky Way. It is one of a hundred million galaxies. It is 800,000 light-years away. It consists of one hundred billion suns, each larger than our own sun."

Then, after a moment of silence, Theodore Roosevelt would grin and say, "Now, I think we are small enough. Let's go to bed."

In this Tranquilizer Era of the Phenobarbital Age we need some of the trustful spirit that stems from a recognition of our smallness resting in God's greatness.

# *AUTUMN THOUGHTS*

*Twenty-one*

# MEANINGFUL CONVERSATION

IF YOU WILL STAND outdoors on these chill autumn evenings, you may chance to hear the distant conversation of migrating birds as they call to each other through the darkness. Sometimes the muted honks of wild geese drift down from a moonlit sky. Again the thin, high pipings of Southbound warblers greet an attentive ear. Bell-like voices of myriad species of feathered travelers set the heavens atingle with vital communications that keep individual birds from getting lost from the flock. It is as if these pilgrims were reminding each other that no one need be lonely. "We are all together. No one need make this hard journey alone. We are at each other's side to guide, to help, and to cheer."

Human beings need something of this deep native wisdom and grace of migrating birds, the wisdom and grace to use their powers of communication for good, for maintaining fellowship, for strengthening faltering spirits, for cheerful purposes.

How often our conversation is meaningless and inconsequential! When William Gillette, the actor, was a young man, he lived in a boardinghouse. At that time he was studying stenography and thought it a good idea to practice shorthand evenings while sitting in the drawing room with other boarders and listening to their conversation. So one evening after another he took down every word spoken by the guests. Mr. Gillette, referring to this experience, one time told a friend, "Years later I went over my notebooks, and found that in four months of incessant conversation, no one had said anything that made any difference to anybody."

How long has it been since you were engaged in a conversation that made a real difference to you? Or, more important still, how long since you said anything that made a real difference in anyone else?

On these fall nights, as migrating birds speed across the uncharted skies, communication is carried on as if their lives

depended upon it. It is the way they keep together and are heartened for their long journey.

Here is a spiritual exercise worthy of your highest effort. Try for one week to communicate with your fellow-men as if their hope and cheer and very lives depended upon what you had to say.

Try it. You can be at least as good as a bird.

*Twenty-two*

# WHAT IS BEHIND IT ALL?

AUTUMN IS FULL of reminders that much that is most vital and real in life cannot be seen. We see only things. But behind the things are the silent, invisible forces that make things possible and that make them significant.

During these days and nights of falling leaves wild Canada geese drift southward. Goose-talk floats down upon the crisp autumn air, the honking voices of winged prophets warning earth-dwellers of coming winter. Look sharply upon a clear fall night, and sometimes you can see across the moon's bright face a thin, unstable, moving procession forming a broad V, then straggling out into a swaying, wavering, single line. From northern Canada they come, from the Barren Grounds near the Arctic, from Labrador and the northernmost outreaches of the United States. Few sights are so filled with the atmosphere of wilderness and few sounds so wild, as the wing-to-wing flight of Canada geese and their gabbling and honking on a late October's night.

The big birds in migration are a thrilling sight. So is the harvest moon that brushes soft light upon their beating wings and tints the tops of rising and falling hills far below, and spreads a silken sheen across little streams and the lakes' broad waters. But beyond sight, and just as real as the observable, are the invisible powers that make for goose-flight and moonlight, and without which neither would be possible. The migration urge is non-material. It cannot be seen or touched or weighed. The moon's soft glow is but the reflection of the sun, say the astronomers – the sun hidden behind the earth's bulk and shining elsewhere now, on the other side of the world, but not here. Moonlight is the visible manifestation of an invisible power.

When, at the dawning of another day, the now concealed sun shows its face again we shall see but a bright round ball in the heavens and nothing of its real power. Is there the faintest hint, as you look at that beneficent globe, that it is really a terrifying cauldron of flames and gases, 865,000 miles in diameter? Does it appear so hot that some celestial pourer could empty the Atlantic, Pacific, and Indian Oceans, and our own Great Lakes, too, into it and they would almost instantly be converted to vapor without even a spit or sputter? The sun is that vast and that hot. Moreover, like all other things, the sun is composed of atoms, invisible particles of matter made up of invisible neutrons and protons spinning in invisible orbits around an invisible nucleus. That bright, round ball in the sky is a symbol of the deceptiveness of appearances. Things are not what they appear to be. Everything is more than a thing. It is a manifestation of an invisible power.

A wedding ring is more than a ring. It is an outward and material sign of an invisible bond of affection, unseen but real. A warm hand-clasp is more than the touch of flesh upon flesh. It is a visible sign of an invisible friendly feeling.

You are invisible. You can see your hand and your foot, but they are not the real you. Your hands and feet move at the impulse of your purpose, your love, your intellect and thought. These make up the real you. Look into the mirror, and what do you see? Your body, but not your character and personality. The power behind that body is the real you, and that power no one on earth has ever seen.

So with all the things we fear and love the most. They are essentially invisible. We see war and its devastation upon cities and hamlets and returning soldiers, sailors, and airmen. But its real ruination is wrought upon the unseen, distraught minds and blighted spirits of mankind, just as its real causes are in the imperceptible suspicions, covetousness, fear, and hatred of man. Munitions and material ravages of war are but visible signs of invisible conditions.

Houses are visible, but homes are not. Churches can be seen, but the fellowship of believers that makes the Church is an invisible spirit. Citizenship papers are seeable, touchable, and weighable, but patriotism is not. A marriage license is purchasable, but love is not. Birthday and anniversary gifts can be measured in terms of dollars and cents, but thoughtfulness and appreciation cannot.

The stupidity and tragedy of materialism lie in being de-

ceived by appearances, which are subject to quick change and decay, and in any case are apt to be misleading. Always man has tried to preserve his material possessions against the ravages of time, and has been disappointed. In the meantime, man's ideas, seemingly so fragile and ephemeral, have outlasted his most durable ornaments, architecture, monuments, tombs, and sacred vessels. Our longing and searching for peace persists after blockbusters have done their worst. Art lingers long after pictures have been lost or destroyed. The Word of God outlasts the writer and his manuscripts. Worship survives the falling of altars and temples. The products of man which time has proven most durable have been his heroic conduct, his inspirations and his ideas, all of which are spiritual.

We all want to be of durable stuff. Our one chance lies in linking our lives to values that outlast our bodies and to the Power that is "behind it all."

*Twenty-three*

# THE POWER OF WAITING

THROUGHOUT the entire range of the animal kingdom, from the lowest, simplest creatures to the highest, we can trace a growing capacity to wait for the basic hungers to be satisfied. The microscopic one-celled amoeba bumps into a food particle. Instantly it surrounds the particle and absorbs it. There is no waiting period between stimulus and response. An earthworm eats its way through the soil, with no preliminaries of sighting food at a distance and then going after it. The earthworm never needs to wait for his meals. They are always in the lumps of earth next to him. He but opens his mouth and they are his.

But the solemn-eyed great horned owl that hoots across our moonlit meadow bears all the marks of a creature fashioned for waiting. His big, saucerlike eyes signify the interval that exists between the onslaught of hunger pains and satisfaction of appetite. First his food – deermouse, snowshoe rabbit or ruffed grouse – is seen at a distance. Then he must spread his wings and launch himself in the direction of his prey. Before the warm, live flesh becomes his supper he must stretch his needle-sharp hooked talons and grasp and kill his victim. Only then can this pirate of the night sky sate his hunger. An owl is equipped by nature for putting up with preliminaries – for waiting.

A snowshoe rabbit's sensitive nose is for smelling food, as well as danger, at a distance. An interval exists between sensing and satisfaction. The fox's strong legs and padded feet are for hunting and stalking his prey – which means waiting. The fox squirrel's storage of acorns, hickory and beech nuts against winter's scarcity implies a still greater waiting period between preparation and gratification. The higher animals are those that must observe preliminaries. They are the creatures who can wait.

The highest animal of all, man, is the creature with the greatest capacity for waiting for his desires to be satisfied.

When man is at his best, he has patience. When he is at his worst, he is impatient.

The honest laborer, working for his living, slowly accumulates his possessions, believing that at last his efforts will be rewarded. The trickster, the gambler, the ardent believer in luck, and the crook contrive to bypass all preliminaries and to get what they want, immediately. They want to take short cuts. What a robber tries to do in a moment's time with a gun at a bank-teller's window, the workman does with prolonged toil. Both are after money and what money can buy. But what a difference in the way they seek it! Of course, patience is not the only difference between them. But it is a significant one.

Two women lie on adjacent beds in a hospital room. Both suffer pain. Both face days of uncertainty. And, at best, both are confronted with a long convalescence. But what a world of difference in their attitudes! Although both are served by the same doctors and nurses and have the same surroundings, one is fretful, depressed, and complaining; and the other is radiant. When one is asked how long she will be in bed she crankily replies, "Forever, I suppose, if I don't get better care than this!" But when the other is asked how long she must remain in the hospital she cheerfully responds, "Only a day at a time." The difference? Primarily one of patience, the capacity to wait.

Patience with preliminaries is found among the highest types of character in the mating relationship. In primitive society there was no need for waiting, no need for courtship nor for consent of the partner nor for a ceremonial wedding. Satisfaction of the mating instinct was almost immediate, as it is among cattle, dogs, sparrows, and rats. Present-day casual sex relationships, the quick taking and shedding of sex partners, are reversions. They show an absence of civilized restraint. They are bestial. The finest homes are founded upon patience, the capacity to wait until physical attraction grows into companionship, or until an angry word dies on the tongue, stillborn, or until a stormy disagreement blows over and there follows a quietness conducive to reflection, penitence, and forgiveness. Happy homes are built of blocks of patience.

Waiting is one of the distinguishing marks of a civilized mind. Probably no development in human history was more important than when some early man or woman planted a seed in the ground and waited to see what would happen. That was the beginning of agriculture.

Some years ago, during the construction of the East River bridges in New York, the engineers were perplexed and frustrated by an old sunken barge that lay imbedded on the river bottom. Efforts had been made to remove the obstruction by using giant steel cables pulled by powerful engines, but to no avail. Derricks wouldn't work. Nothing that was tried succeeded. Then a young man fresh from engineering school begged permission to try an idea. He waited for low tide and then had a large barge towed to a spot directly over the sunken derelict. Then he ordered divers to tie cables between the floating barge and the submerged wreckage. When this had been done he and his men stood back and waited. Slowly and quietly the mighty tides of the great Atlantic came into the East River, silently lifting the floating barge and with it the sunken boat. The young engineer had hitched his task to the powerful Atlantic tides, and waited. Patience is often just that – waiting for God's tides to take hold.

A prattling woman one time approached the Polish pianist, Ignace Paderewski, after a concert at which he had played. She cooed, "Oh, Mr. Paderewski, you must have had a world of patience to learn to play as you do."

"It's not that at all, my dear woman," replied Paderewski. "I have no more patience than anyone else. It's just that I use mine."

Like our animal brothers, the owl and rabbit and fox squirrel, we are equipped for waiting. Everyone has some patience. The best people use theirs.

*Twenty-four*

# WHEN BURNED

YOU CAN KNOW wood thoroughly only after you have burned it. Hidden beneath the bark are secrets that only burning will reveal. There lie the tars and creosote, acetone and ethylene, resins and gums, wood oil and wood alcohol, acetic acid and sugars, and a variety of confined gases. Flame unlocks the prison cells and sets these hidden captives free.

Fire is a revealer. It tells us what was there all along, but unknown. It manifests characteristics of wood that remain concealed until log becomes fuel. Then each wood burns with characteristic flame. Each emits its own individual aroma. Each finds, at last, its voice and crackles, sighs, or softly murmurs, according to its temperament.

Impregnated with resins, gums, and oils, spruce and pine logs burn with a fierce flame and a sharp crackling.

Elm, heavy with moisture and slow to dry no matter how long it is weathered after cutting, sobs and blubbers and sheds watery tears as it burns.

Balsam and hemlock, spruce and tamarack are exhibitionists, wildly celebrating their demise as they carelessly throw sparks all around as if to take the whole world with them when they go.

Paper birch spouts a vivid yellow flame, and apple wood furnishes a multicolored light.

The blaze of hickory is nearly the hottest of any American wood. Indians taught our pioneering forebears to use hickory in preference to any other of the abundant woods found here in this new land. So they did, for heating their cabins and smoking their hams and roasting their shins.

All woods reveal something thus far hidden about themselves when they are burned.

What fire does for wood a crisis does for character. A crisis is character's opportunity to express its hidden nature. No one knows or shows his real colors while life is pleasant, easy, and comfortable. Under stress, whatever that strain might be, the human spirit manifests its weaknesses and strengths.

Perhaps this is one reason a good God allows suffering in His world: it is the only way we can find out what we really are.

*Twenty-five*

# IN SPOTS

AUTUMN COMES to the North in spots rather than simultaneously. A part of creation is still in the midst of spring — as are the shaggy-mane mushrooms, which magically make an appearance in pastures and waste places now, as morel mushrooms did in the month of May. Some plants are flowering in October as if it were their summertime — Jerusalem artichoke, blue gentian, ladies' tresses, asters, and goldenrod being among them. But here and there, in spots and patches, autumn is making itself felt. The whitetail fawns are losing their spots and the adult deer are shedding their summer coats and replacing them with winter garb. Chipmunks are retreating to their winter homes and settling down to a long, deathlike sleep. Moles dig deeper into the earth, below the frost line. Ferns turn brown and die. Drone and worker bees expire and bumblebee queens find winter quarters well protected from freezing temperatures. Leaves turn color. Berries and nuts ripen. Brook trout spawn. Squirrels gather and store acorns and hickory nuts. Here and there, amidst the remnants of summer, there are signs of fall and of forthcoming winter. Autumn is here — in spots.

The best things of life, like autumn, come to us in spots. Knowledge does, friendship does, and so does happiness. The longer one lives and the wiser one grows, the more capable he becomes of accepting and adjusting to this partial, incomplete nature of life. In early childhood we are impatient with incompleteness. We ask questions like: "Where is God?" "What does God look like?" "Why do things change all the time?" "Why do people who do wrong get punished?" "Why doesn't God give me everything I want?" "Why do people die?" And we are seldom satisfied with the answers. We pile on the "why's" until parents, running out of knowledge and patience, tell us to "run along now and play." But the incomplete answers frustrate and fret us. We demand satisfaction. "But why?" we persist. Later, as we mature, we learn that no one has all the answers to our questions.

Our knowledge is spotty. It is not all-encompassing. Our world cannot be fully explained. Here and there we have a hint of what the universe means. We see in the regular rising and setting of the sun and the predictable ebb and flow of the tides that this universe is orderly and not capricious or whimsical. We know something of the mixed complexity and simplicity of life here, the hundreds of thousands of different species of life, yet all made of only about one hundred elements and all functioning on a few basic principles, such as eating, growing, moving, and reproducing themselves. But in every realm, before we have gone far, we pass over the borders of knowledge and into the domain of mystery. A leading biologist declared a short time ago that biologists do not thoroughly understand even one biological reaction. Thomas Edison, emphasizing how limited science is in its outreach into the mysterious, one time said, "We don't know the millionth part of one percent about anything. We don't know what water is. We don't know what light is. We don't know what gravitation is. We don't know what enables us to keep on our feet when we stand up. We don't know what electricity is. We don't know what heat is. We don't know anything about magnetism. We have a lot of hypotheses about these things, but that is all." Edison did not mean we know nothing about anything. Rather, he was saying that the ultimate, complete, and final answers are elusive. As Saint Paul put it, "Now we see through a glass darkly. . . . We know in part." We know in spots.

We are friends in spots. Do you know any human being of whom you wholeheartedly approve, any person who is thoroughly perfect? Do you have a friend whose mind and heart are entirely exposed to you, with whom you agree on every issue, big or little, whose likes and dislikes are in all ways identical with your own? No, friendship means agreement on some matters, but not in everything; the sharing of some interests, but not all; a basic understanding, but not complete understanding. If we look far enough and deeply enough we will find in those we love most an area of mystery and one of disagreement and another of imperfection. There can never be a complete union of minds. We are friends at certain points and in patches.

We are happy in spots. To complain because we are not altogether, thoroughly happy is the height of foolishness. Everyone, even the wealthiest man on earth, can think of something he still lacks. The man or woman who is most blissfully married can find some fault somewhere in the marriage partner. The most successful worker can find some distasteful element in his task. If you have some meaningful purpose to work for, someone to love, a few friends, a God to worship and obey, a clear conscience, and all of life's barest necessities, you can be grateful, even though you are not altogether happy. Nobody is. The happiest person is happy only in spots.

Autumn's progress gives us a clue as to what we can all profitably do. Autumn is spreading, from one spot to another, until at last there will be only a few places where it has not reached – like the sheltered nooks where insects still live, and the deep holes of the earth to which many creatures have fled for warmth, and the depths of Lake Michigan where the temperature remains the same summer and winter. It will never be thoroughly autumn everywhere, but the season is growing upon us. The spots of autumn are enlarging.

So must we grow, expanding our knowledge, our friendship with God and man, and our capacity for happiness.

*Twenty-six*

# THE BREVITY OF LIFE

DEER-HUNTING SEASON arrives this week. Once more we shall hear the roar of rifles in the woods and the triumphant shouts of excited hunters who have bagged their game, and here and there we shall see the strung-up bodies of whitetails that a few hours before throbbed with life. While I know full well that in many northern areas deer must be killed or they will starve, and while I am no gushing sentimentalist, still I never see a dead deer but that I feel a twinge of regret.

One thing that bothers me about deer hunting is that most deer are brought to such an early death by the hunters' guns. A deer's natural life span is above fifteen years, and many a deer has been kept in captivity for well over eighteen years. But it is a lucky one indeed that attains ten years in the wild. And where hunting pressure is intense, most deer shot will be less than five years of age, which means that these graceful, vivacious animals die when they have lived about a third of their natural life expectancy. It is somewhat as if most human beings in our locality died violently before they were twenty-three years old.

Life is brief enough at its best. For the bear it is a span of only twenty to thirty years, for the fox less than a decade, about the same for a gray squirrel, ten to fifteen years for the wolf, and a mere three years for the white-footed mouse. But then the violence of their natural enemies and the predation of man reduce their lives still more. The moral of all this is not that man should not hunt, but rather that when he does take his gun into forest and field it should be to hunt sparingly rather than greedily, intelligently and appreciatively rather than bloodthirstily, knowing that the lithe bundle of vitality he reduces to lifeless flesh will likely have lived only about one third of its years. There are haunts it will never visit, streams from which it will never drink again, offspring it will never sire. The hunter has contributed to the brevity of life.

The brevity of life is one of its obvious characteristics. Each form of living thing has its own limitations upon longevity. No deer lives to be ninety years of age as does many a human being, nor does any mouse live to the age of eighteen as do some deer, and no May fly attains the age of three as do meadow mice. No human life span has reached three thousand years as do sequoia trees in California. Human life seems brief, no matter its length, if a person lives with enjoyment and packs his days full of interest and plans for the future. When some people die it does not seem to be much of a tragedy, because they never really lived. They were grumpy rather than joyful. They existed in the past rather than in the present and the future. They would not know what to do with the tomorrows if their lives had been prolonged. But for others almost any span of existence offered them would be too short, because there would always be more to accomplish, more good to be done, more hope and cheer to spread around.

Some of our greatest thrills and excitements stem from the limitations life imposes upon us. A football team does not have all day to score against its opponent. The teams have only an hour of playing time. If a team is six points behind its opponent, and on the march toward the adversary's goal line, and there is only one-half minute left in the game, excitement rises to delirium. If the time were then extended from one-half minute to one-half day, interest in the game would immediately subside. Limitations provoke fascination. The baseball batter is allowed but three strikes. Grant each player two dozen strikes each turn at bat and the game would become unbearably tiresome. The real fun in the game is derived from the limitations imposed upon the players.

Religious people sense the challenge life flings at mankind in the form of restrictions. In the Ninetieth Psalm the writer presents a sobering, doleful thought: "The days of our years are threescore years and ten; and if by reason of strength they be fourscore years, yet is their strength labour and sorrow; for it is soon cut off, and we fly away." A solemn reflection, isn't it? But the Psalmist continues toward a conclusion that has adventure in it: "So teach us to number our days, that we may apply our hearts unto wisdom." The Scripture writer felt the pressure of life's limitations. He knew his physical resources were not boundless. He would not live

forever here. The Almighty Umpire has placed a time limit on the game of life. Very well, then, that is what makes our days interesting. They are not interminable. All that we do must be accomplished before the period is over. Every score must be effected before the bell tolls. That adds excitement and interest to our days.

Not only do time boundaries add zest to our lives, but our days take on additional meaning, too, when brevity is recognized. When the wise know their time is limited they are apt to use it more carefully. Mind you, I say "use it," not "save it." We time-conscious Americans are forever trying to "save time." We use an automobile rather than walk to "save time," and we have our automobiles geared to drive at ridiculous, high speeds – to "save time." We have invented a vast number of gadgets for kitchen, shop, and office that are advertised to "save time." Yet no one ever saves time, not if we mean by saving it, hoarding it, as some people do string and others money. All the time you are given today you will spend before midnight – every bit of it. Cut all the corners you please, live at a furious rate, race through every moment of the day, and still you cannot save a moment for use tomorrow. All of today's minutes must be spent before midnight. Time can be squandered, spent foolishly, or spent wisely. But somehow, somewhere, it must be *spent*. It cannot be saved.

Consciousness of the brevity of time leads some of us to spend it foolishly. "Since life is short, live it up," some people say. Live it hilariously, seeking pleasure as the greatest good. Don't take life so seriously, the proponents of this view contend, for none of us have much time. Life is so short! Spend it freely! That is like a farmer saying that because he has only ten acres of land, instead of six hundred as does his neighbor, therefore it does not matter what he does with his ten acres. Rather, if he owns so little, it is all the more imperative that he make the best possible use of his limited land resources. The argument in favor of squandering life because it is short is like a man who has lost a million dollars and is down to his last ten, saying, "After all, it is only ten dollars! It doesn't matter what I do with that little amount." Rather, *because* ten dollars is all he has, he must see that he makes it count. If his money were unlimited he could afford to be somewhat prodigal. But with so little he had better invest it carefully.

Have you heard it said, "You are young only once," as an

excuse for living carelessly? Youth will not last forever, why not spend one's early days wildly? No intelligent young person ever falls for that line of argument. It is *because* childhood and adolescence are brief that they ought not be wasted. These are the impressionable, formative years when patterns of feeling, thinking, and acting are established. It is the growing period of life. No youngster will ever grow so much again, change so much again, nor be so impressionable again. Because one is young only once he ought to see to it that his mind is exposed to the highest thoughts, the best friendships, and that he eats and drinks of the good things of life that make for future courage, hope, loyalty, cheerfulness, and service.

Where did we get the expression, "The dangerous forties"? It comes from the long experience of the race where many a generation has seen the middle-aged behave more foolishly than when they were young. People in their forties see their youth slipping away. Women fear their glamor is disappearing. Men find beltlines enlarging, hair vanishing, and athletic prowess waning. So in their forties people are bound to be tempted. They want to see if they have the same old zip, the same sex appeal. Flirtations are frequent. Many a man and woman who in early years were above moral reproach and whose loyalty in early marriage was unquestioned, fall in middle age because they fear powers are diminishing, glamor is going, and they are stunned with a consciousness of the shortness of life.

If life is so short we must be all the more careful of its use. Middle age should be one of life's most satisfying periods. With the uncertainties, giddiness, and instability of youth left behind, and with the physical liabilities of old age not yet arrived, middle age can be the bright noon of life. The wise person will handle his middle years in a thrifty fashion.

Aging people feel the brevity of years more than do most others. Growing old is not so bad if we consider the only alternative, but it is troublesome enough if we still have much we would like to accomplish, and vigor is diminishing, and life's brief day is nearing sunset time. Then, especially, we should give our time to the things that matter most. The fact that "the time is short" can be a stimulant rather than a depressive. At seventy-four Emanuel Kant wrote his finest philosophical works. When he was eighty, Verdi produced *Falstaff* and five years later his hauntingly beautiful "Ave Maria." Goethe was eighty when he completed *Faust* and Tennyson eighty when he wrote "Crossing the Bar." Michelangelo finished his greatest work at eighty-seven and Titian painted the historic picture, "Battle of Lepanto," at ninety-eight. A consciousness of a limited future brought forth the best efforts of these servants of humankind. It should in all the aged. As long as an old person has a single human contact left there is good to be done. And scoring within the time limit can be as sporting and thrilling as in any other game our years have offered.

No matter our age or situation, what can anyone of us do about the brevity of life? We can remember that if life is short we have time only for the best. Among our good public servants are the junk man and the garbage man. They get rid of refuse, trash, and clutter, helping us to simplify life by carting away the unimportant stuff, the useless. But they can only carry off what we set out for them in the trash and garbage cans. The choice is ours. We need an improved sense of discrimination, knowing what is worth discarding and what should be kept. Since life is too small to hold everything, what shall we keep? Since most of us have limited time for reading, what shall we read – the great books about great men, great spirits, great facts and problems? If a person could read all day every day he could afford to peruse third-rate literature, but with limited time for reading we need to choose the best.

Life is too brief for grumpy fault-finding and carping criticism, too short for grudges, malice, and revenge, too fleeting for indulgence in the things that death so quickly snatches away. Our days are just roomy enough to accommodate the gifts that time cannot corrode – like faith, hope, and love.

Live each day in grateful wonder as if it were the first day you had ever seen, and live each day thoughtfully and effectively as if it were the last you would ever see.

*Twenty-seven*

# UNFINISHED BUSINESS

WHEN I LOOK around me on the natural world I am impressed with the realization that everything I see once existed only in the realm of possibility. The long, lush grasses near the lake shore were once but seeds. Tall trees that grace the shore line were once but maple seeds carried by the wind on smooth, winged, incurved double planes, or little winged nutlets dropped by birches, or seeds hidden in the cones of spruce, hemlock, and balsam fir. Timid deer that haunt our shores at sundown and daybreak were once but microscopic germs of life that resembled grown whitetails in no way whatsoever.

This world is full of incompleteness. At most well-ordered business meetings there comes a moment when the chairman asks, "Is there any unfinished business?" Often there is. But in the agenda of life there is always unfinished business. There are seeds meant to become grasses and trees whose destiny is yet unfulfilled, and there are the germ seeds of future deer that must continue to develop for months to come before more wide-eyed fawns can skip and frolic across the sunlit glades in our woods. Wherever one looks in nature there are latencies to be developed into actualities, seeds of the future alive with possibilities.

The potentials latent in people caught Jesus' attention and fascinated Him. He recognized seeds of goodness that no one else saw, and by His encouragement He helped the sleeping possibilities to awaken and grow into established realities. He saw in Matthew the tax gatherer all the avarice that was there, but something else, too – a dissatisfaction with what he was and an aspiration to be better. He found in Mary Magdalene a longing for purity. Nobody else guessed she was capable of that. He discerned in Simon a sturdiness of soul that was hidden from more casual eyes. He saw what God sees: not only what man is, but what he is capable of becoming.

In one of George MacDonald's stories a character cries in wild frustration, "I do not see why God ever made me," to which her friend responds, "God hasn't made you yet. He is making you and you don't like it." We sometimes wish that when we were born the whole man and the whole woman could have emerged into completeness. But as it is we are not born once and for all, but again and again. When an infant comes into the world he is incomplete. His head is born, but not his imagination. That must develop. His heart is born, but not his affections. They will come later. His feet are born, but not the goals of life toward which he will strive. A newly born babe is unfinished business. We all are.

Some of us need patience. God won't send it to us full grown and well developed. We all have within us seedlike possibilities of this grace. If we want more than that we shall need to feed what patience we have, and exercise it so that it can grow. There is enough frustration and disappointment already in the lives of most of us upon which we could exercise our little patience if we would. The difference between an irritable, flustered person and a long-suffering, forbearing one is not usually the amount of patience they had when born. One has nurtured his patience on life's plentiful adversities. The other has not.

When one becomes a follower of the Master, he is still a long way from being a complete Christian. Many have chosen to be Christians for reasons of fear. They have been frightened into it as a kind of escape from hell. Some have become Christians for selfish reasons, seeking a reward of heaven. Selfishness that is blessed with the name of religion is selfishness still. There is some unfinished business such people need to attend to, growing beyond fear and selfishness and into loving God for God's sake rather than for their own benefit alone.

Just as in the dormant seed there rests a plan for the mature tree and within the embryo there is hidden a pattern of what the grown animal will be, so within every child of God there are traces of what is expected of us, the tiniest inclinations toward goodness, a bit of hunger for God, at least some desire to count in the world. The chief goal of life is to become, under God, what we are capable of becoming, developing all the latent possibilities.

The Brooklyn Bridge was built while its architect, Roebling, was sick in bed. While he was unable to watch the construction of the project, he did send advice to the contractors from his sick room. When the great structure was finally finished, friends propped Roebling with pillows in a half-reclining position in a small boat and maneuvered the boat into a favorable position in the East River beneath the vast span of steel and concrete. There the architect lay for a long time, looking from the bridge to the blueprints he held in his hands and then back to the bridge again. After a long silence, Roebling sank back into the comfort of the pillows with a smile of satisfaction and exclaimed, "It is like the plan."

One of the highest contributions of Jesus Christ to mankind has been that of providing a blueprint of what life should be like. And a supreme satisfaction would be to come to the end of a single day and to look from our work of life-building to Him and be able to say, "It is like the plan."

*Twenty-eight*

# A PRAYER OF THANKS ON A STARLIT EVENING

LORD of heaven and earth,
Many are the blessings which I have within my reach –

Food for eating,
Clothes for wearing,
A house for shelter,
And loved ones near enough to touch.
They are all needed.
They are all good.
For each I offer daily thanks.
But on this starlit night
I lift my praise for all those things
I prize without possessing, like
The stars above,
The world's priceless art,
The skills of those whose bright gifts dim my poor lights.
For all the beauty and all the goodness beyond my reach
I thank Thee, O Lord.
Amen.

# *WINTER THOUGHTS*

*Twenty-nine*

# ALL WEATHERS MAKE A SOUL

AT FIRST GLANCE winter's severe cold and bluster seem to be the enemies of all vegetable and animal growth. In the late fall "killing frosts" play a dismal prelude to a chilling theme of snows and blizzards, sleet and ice. Leaves wither and fall. Flowers droop. Woodchucks and chipmunks retreat to their dens in the earth. Wasps desert their paper nests and take refuge in tree holes and roof corners. Many birds wing southward. Frogs and toads burrow into the mud of pond bottoms. Fishes decrease their activity. To all appearances winter is the enemy of nature from which life flees or else perishes.

But appearances are deceiving. When winter lies inch-thick upon our window sills, when northwesterly winds whip stinging sleet around our venerable, bare-limbed beech inside Hidden Brook gate, when deer once more embroider the snowy coverlet on our acreage with dainty, heart-shaped tracks and dig for beech mast there and search for frozen apples over yonder—life will still go on, sometimes in spite of winter hardship and often because of it.

In the deep snow many a meadow mouse and white-footed mouse will find shelter from a hawk's fierce gaze and murderous talons. Mice will safely tunnel from nest to buried food and back again unmolested by winged predators.

Cottontail rabbits and snowshoe hares will use banks of snow as ladders for climbing high on shrubs and trees where they can nibble on tender shoots and delectable buds otherwise out of their reach.

A period of penetrating cold is necessary for the proper sprouting of many kinds of seeds, and some species of plants are benefited by the bite of frost. Some years ago, at a mission agricultural farm in India, it was discovered that when the tops of eggplants were frostbitten the plants produced a second crop. (Thereafter, when eggplants had grown a first crop the Indians would not wait for a freeze but imitated the

attack of cold weather by cutting back the plants so that they could produce once more.)

For proper hatching, the eggs of many insects, such as the Rocky Mountain locust, need to pass through a cold period. During the coldest months of the year some creatures will grow so rapidly that when spring arrives they will have passed completely through childhood and adolescence and will be able to take their places as adults. Stone flies and May flies in the brook will make this change during the winter. So will larval salamanders and the tadpoles of green frogs and bullfrogs.

Many fresh-water clams and crayfishes will lay their eggs in the frigid waters of stream and pond during the severest months of winter.

While we commonly think of the kindly warmth of spring and the beneficent heat of summer as providing the only favorable conditions for growth, the truth is that here in the North all weathers have a place in Nature's scheme, and without the sharp austerity of winter some forms of life would not last.

Long ago geographers and anthropologists proved that civilization advances most rapidly in the temperate zones where there is a mixture of weather conditions – summer balminess followed by autumn chill and wintry blasts of wind and snow. The year-round warmth of the tropics makes for spiritual torpor, mental laziness, and physical dullness. It takes all kinds of weather to stimulate men to be at their best.

While we pray for lives full of sunshine and pleasantness, God could do us no greater harm than to answer these prayers, for it takes all kinds of weather to grow a soul. Radiant days are necessary, when bright blessings shine down upon us from above and we absorb providential goodness as a sunny hillside soaks up light. Rainy days are needed when the spirit is refreshed and cleansed as when leaves, grasses, and crops of countless forests and fields drink deeply of heaven's plenty. But wintry cold and snowy blasts from the North are also required in the temperate life – days when our lives are revealingly tested just as hard winds, heavy snows, and slashing sleet prove the strengths and weaknesses of a Northern woods, bowing snow-laden evergreen limbs in humility and breaking rotten branches off all the trees. So life's hard weather demonstrates in us what deserves to last and what ought to fade and die. Only winter clearly shows which trees are evergreen!

All weathers make a soul. It was after blindness descended upon John Milton that he wrote his sublimest poetry. Beethoven's loveliest sonatas were composed after he was stricken with deafness. What would Lincoln be without his lifelong seizures of melancholy? What would Christ be without His cross?

An American tourist in Italy watched a lumberjack at work. As the logs floated down the swift mountain stream the lumberman would thrust his hook into a particular log and draw it aside.

"Those logs all look alike," said the tourist. "Why do you pick out just a few?"

"They are not all alike," the lumberman replied. "Some were grown low on the mountainside where they were protected all their lives from harsh winds. Their grains are coarse. They are good only for lumber, so I let them pass on down the stream to the lumber mills. But a few logs grew on the mountain top. From the time they were tiny seedlings they felt the lashings of high winds and the weight of heavy snows, and they grow strong and tough and fine-grained. We do not use these for ordinary lumber. No, sir! These few are especially selected for choice work."

So God uses wind-buffeted souls for His choicest work.

*Thirty*

# SIGNS OF PROMISE

WHEN SNOW LIES soft and thick upon the ground and ice rests heavily upon the ponds and lakes, when one's steps play a tiny tinkling music upon the trail and every fence post wears a woolly cap and every shrub a tattered white gown, when mischievous, boisterous winds playfully puff little whiffs of snow down a stroller's neck and hungrily gnaw at the icing on the trees, spring seems far away and summer but a faint memory.

But break the ice off the twigs of shrubs and trees and examine them closely enough and you will find delicate buds carefully wrapped in tough, thick scales that protect their tender parts from winter's fierce bite. These buds are Nature's reminders that her care and concern have not been withdrawn, leaving all the creatures of the North everlastingly at winter's mercy. Buds are summer wrapped in winter, ready to unfold when the proper moment arrives.

These hidden buds remind me of flag signals flown in the days when sailing vessels plowed the high seas. Three signal flags, "B. N. C." meant, "I will not abandon you!" When a ship was in distress nothing was so heartening as to see a sister ship draw alongside flying that signal. It meant hope. It rekindled courage, and bore the promise of more life to come to sailors who faced imminent death. So in nature, now, buds are promises of more life to come. We are not deserted by an unfeeling Creator to the crippling brutalities of wind, snowdrifts, sleet, and ice. Spring is on its way. Every snow-and-ice-covered bud witnesses to that prophetic hope.

As in nature, so in life, everywhere I go I see signs of hope as if God were hanging out signals that say, "I will not abandon you."

Every time I see a newborn baby through the nursery window at the hospital I take hope. God is not through with the race. He is still making tomorrow's men and women.

There are around us now hopeful signs that God may yet

bring us to a warless world. For the first time in history the masses of people have a sensitive conscience about war. Earlier in the history of the human race war was celebrated grandly. It was welcomed with fanatical frenzy and was thought to be the will of God. In fact, the Almighty was pictured as a God of War. But not now. There is a growing will for peace among men and a rising conviction that the war method of solving international disputes is morally wrong and shameful. We still have a long way to go before we learn to live peaceably with one another, but, like buds on sleet-covered trees, the signs of hope are here in the emerging conviction that war is wrong and that the final battle of nations must be a war on war itself.

In this life there are hopeful signs of the life hereafter. Look at it this way: Isn't it true of most of us that the more we learn the more we want to learn, and the better we become the sharper our appetite grows for greater goodness? We have a craving for knowledge and goodness that is never satisfied here. But just as our bodies' hunger for food can eventually be satisfied, if not by a cracker, then by a steak dinner, and our need for sleep can be satisfied, if not by a cat nap, then possibly by a full night and day in bed, so if our desire for knowledge and goodness cannot be answered by this life, it can be in the life to come. There is somewhere a satisfaction for every human craving. And our very yearning for a better and more complete life than earth affords is a sign of a more abundant life ahead.

This list of hopeful signs could be greatly lengthened, taking in countless circumstances and situations. There are no hopeless situations. There are only hopeless people who fail to see the signs of promise. Beyond every dark night there dawns a tomorrow. On the other side of every wilderness there is a promised land. Beyond every winter there is a spring.

*Thirty-one*

# NEED

ONE DISTINGUISHING MARK of all living things is that they have needs. Non-living things do not. At least I cannot imagine the rocks that rim our shore needing anything. Nothing seems to matter to them; sunshine or rain, high water or low, summer or winter, they remain strangely unaffected. But all living creatures have needs—needs that are constant and urgent.

Even in winter, that period of the year when all the North that is not dead seems half asleep, there is this clear difference between the non-living and the living things of the ice-glazed and snow-covered earth: the non-living have no needs; the living do. Dead trees need no moisture. Living ones do. It will make no vital difference to the non-living snow if temperatures drop to 20 below zero and remain there for ten days, but such an event would mean dire suffering to the whitetail deer and death to many of the tribe of wild birds that can stand bitter cold for a few hours, but not for a prolonged period. The sunken logs and sand on the bottom of a small lake will not perish if the lake freezes over, but if ice and snow cover the water for a long time water plants will perish. Lacking light for photosynthesis, plants die and decompose, flooding the lake with carbon dioxide, depleting the oxygen supply and winter-killing the fish. Unless their needs are satisfied all things die.

This disposition of living matter to insist upon having its needs met is well recognized by biologists and used by them to control unwanted forms of life such as fungi, bacteria, and weeds. Bread mold, a kind of fungus, needs moisture to thrive. One way to discourage the mold is to keep bread in a dry place. Heating the bread will destroy the fungus. When its need for dampness is frustrated the fungus dies.

Some fungi and bacteria love oxygen and cool places, hence much food is protected from them by heating them in cans from which oxygen has been expelled. Unable to obtain the oxygen they require, and being heated above a tolerable temperature, these enemies of man's food supply are destroyed. When their needs are not met they perish.

Harmful weeds are killed by depriving them of their needs. They require roots for obtaining moisture and nutriment from the soil. The most old-fashioned way of destroying weeds is to pull them up by the roots, depriving them of these necessities of life. Recently, plant poisons have been developed that kill weeds by striking at other necessities, such as upsetting the nutrient balance and causing plants either to starve themselves or to indulge in overgrowth, both of which are fatal. Always, a plant's needs are met, or it dies.

One mark of a vital, living spirit is that it has needs, recognizes them, and seeks to satisfy them. Just as a living body is one that still has requirements, a living soul is one that has recognized need.

The urgency of having a need and being aware of it is seen in the fact that in every important matter a felt need precedes great experience. How long has it been since your mind dwelt on geometry, calculus, and trigonometry? Months? Years? Perhaps you have never given any thought to these matters. If not, it was because there was no need to do so. But the engineers who planned the Mackinac Bridge thought almost constantly about higher mathematics, because the building of the bridge made such thinking necessary. Before the bridge could be built someone had to make use of higher mathematics.

How long has it been since you last thought of the mechanics of breathing? Hours? Perhaps days? But if a loved one, dearer to you than life itself, should have pronounced difficulty breathing because of pneumonia or a heart ailment, you immediately rush him to a hospital where an oxygen tent is available, and you give much anxious thought to his having enough oxygen in his lungs. We are most conscious of the importance of air when someone dear to us is deprived of it. So with food, education, the church; so with loving-kindness and patience and most things good, their importance is most vividly demonstrated by the lack of them.

One of the chief reasons for irreligion is a lack of a strongly felt need of God, and it is doubtful if anyone ever finds God unless he first senses a need of Him. A shallow person, who has experienced no profoundly disturbing trouble, no burden of guilt, no heartache, no perplexity, no struggling aspirations, no craving for a better life, can hardly be expected to find God, for he will not seek Him. Superficial people may toy with the idea of God, like boys playing with an apparatus, attempting to construct a make-believe wireless telegraphy instrument. But before one can know the importance of wireless telegraphy he needs to be on a storm-battered ship, far out at sea, and desperately needing help. So before one can

sense his need of God he must be made aware of his want of a help greater than anything man can provide.

A consciousness of need prompts great public service. Those who can exist in the midst of humanity's cares and sufferings and remain unmoved, and do not notice the need, or noticing, do not minister to the lack, are already dead. The alive possess a need-awareness. Jane Addams, the badly crippled child of wealthy parents, was once traveling on a London bus with her father. She saw a cabbage fall from a passing wagon and a hungry man fall upon it and ravenously devour it. Jane Addams could never forget the face of that man. Twenty years after she established Hull House in Chicago Miss Addams declared that the cabbage incident in London had awakened in her a consciousness of the privation existing in the world and aroused a determination to do something about it. Whether it is Jane Addams establishing a settlement house in Chicago, Sir Wilfred Grenfell bringing medical aid to the fisher folk of Labrador, or Dr. Albert Schweitzer operating on the stricken black people of French Equatorial Africa, behind every example of public service there lies one indispensable motivation – a recognized need.

The most exciting and stirring sound in the world is a cry for help, and nothing makes one feel so strong as to hear such a call. A call for help has been known to make the timid brave, the non-swimmer risk his life to save a drowning man, the poor divide his last meal to feed a starving child.

And what is religion if it is not this, at least – man's need for help, and God's answer; man's need and God's sufficiency?

*Thirty-two*

# HOW TO HANDLE YOUR HATREDS

SOME SOLEMN and cynical observers of wild life complain of Nature's cruelty. They point to the furious attack of wolf on caribou, of hawk on song sparrow, snake on mouse, and pike on minnow, as examples of the ceaseless terror that visits the kingdom of the wild, and they completely ignore the fact that in a system where animals and plants must die that others might live, there is little if any of the feeling that we know as hatred. As a rule, animals kill other animals not because they hate them but because they must eat to live. And the violent deaths that are necessary in this scheme are nearly never prolonged, but almost always mercifully sudden, painless, and easy. In the strictest sense of the word, "cruelty" implies enjoying seeing another's pain, and among even the highest animals such cruelty is nearly non-existent. Cruel hostility is an attitude of which man almost alone is capable.

Psychologists generally agree that feelings of hostility get their start in childhood and stem from the inevitable frustrations children meet on their way toward maturity. Very early in his life the child learns the meaning of the words "No," "You mustn't," and "You'll have to wait a while." He becomes irritated by restraints put upon him, angered at those who hold him in check, control him, and repress him. But since the feeling of frustration can seldom be freely expressed by striking back at his parents and bigger brothers and sisters, it is repressed and diffused throughout his subconscious mind and is later revealed in less direct and more unwholesome ways. Since we have all been somewhat controlled and suppressed in childhood, we all have some feelings of hostility either plainly shown in our conduct or deeply hidden in our natures.

Hostility is not a new problem. It is as old as the human race. The earliest known picture drawn by prehistoric man shows men killing one another. The Bible doesn't move far from its opening sentence before it tells the story of Cain murdering his brother Abel. The ancient Romans promoted circuses where condemned men and women were confined in an arena with wild beasts and torn to bits before a fascinated audience. And the history of Christianity is blotted with the blood of Christians murdered by other Christians because they deviated at some point from the orthodox position.

It would be bad enough if our expressions of hatred hurt our fellow-men, but what compounds our misery is that the hostile person is always a victim of his own feelings. He inevitably sips from the cup by which he hoped to poison another. Some years ago on the "Amos and Andy" radio program Andy was repeatedly irritated by a big, exuberant acquaintance who would heartily slap Andy across the chest whenever they chanced to meet. Andy got "fed up" and devised a plan. He related to Amos what he had in mind: "I'm fixed for him! I put a stick of dynamite in my vest pocket. The next time he slaps me on the chest he's going to get his hand blown off!" He didn't seem to realize that at the moment the man's hand was blown off, Andy's chest would be shattered to bits. But that is the way it is with hatred. The one who hates is hurt worse than the one being hated. Hatred disturbs our rest and sleep. It upsets digestion. It erects barriers between ourselves and our fellows, stopping the good they could do us, and — more seriously — hindering the good we could do them. Hatred never builds any good in us, because its nature is destructive rather than constructive. As Joseph Fort Newton once put it, "Hate never builds anything; it can only blast. Every beautiful thing has been loved into being."

Yet, the world's worst people and its best people, alike, have been haters. The criminal is the sort of person who acts out his hostile feelings toward other human beings in a direct manner. He may steal from them, assault them with weapons, or kill them outright. A village gossip vents hostile feelings almost as viciously, but with less severe legal consequences. But gossip, in its way, can be as hateful and destructive as a knife or a gun. The world's worst people employ

their hostility in destroying what is good: human life, another's property, or another's reputation.

The world's best people vent their hatred, too, but upon those things that deserve hating. They are the researchers and doctors who destroy disease, the men and women of insight in management and labor who aim to bring an end to injustice in industry, the educators who uproot ignorance and superstition and plant learning, the peacemakers who work to abolish war, the representatives of religion who seek to destroy evil and help God build a colony of heaven on earth.

The best people hate, but they are discerning in what they hate. On the morning of December 8th, 1941, the day after the Japanese assaulted Pearl Harbor, Marion Forgey Line wrote a meaningful prayer:

"O Lord, let me not
Hate too much.
Let me hate this
Thing called War.
Let me hate the bitter
strife in the hearts of
men
In our own land and afar.
But, oh, Lord, let me not
Hate the people,
Flesh and blood,
Even as we,
The men and the boys
In strange uniforms,
The hungry children,
And lonely wives like me."

Everyone might profitably pray, "O Lord, let me learn to hate the right things." In every community there is enough of life-destroying, personality-crippling evil to absorb all our hostile, destructive instincts. Just as a gardener must not only love flowers, but also despise weeds, so if everyone, everywhere, would learn to hate and uproot the right things, what a garden of God we could plant in their stead!

*Thirty-three*

# ONE SHOT

Stories of the phenomenal shooting accuracy of our pioneering forefathers seem somewhat exaggerated. Some say our forebears laughed at a rifleman and declared him hopelessly clumsy with a gun if he hit a squirrel anywhere else but in the eye when shooting from fifty yards away. While in our time such amazing expertness is found only in circus side shows and movie and television exhibitions, it doubtlessly was common in frontier days.

One reason why early American hunters were so skilled with a long rifle was that they were always in practice. They had to be. At the cabin in the clearing there were hungry mouths to be fed, and the meager crops on the tiny acreage at the forest edge would not supply all the family's wants. So daily the head of the family and the half-grown boys lifted their rifles from crude racks on the cabin wall and stole silently away into the tall timber and spread out to hunt down deer, squirrels, turkeys, or whatever their luck would bring. Daily practice, born of necessity, made skillful riflemen of the frontiersmen.

Not only did an American pioneer enjoy almost constant practice with his gun, but he shot with the intense concentration of a desperate man, as if each shot was the only one he could take at his game. It was "either now or never." The old muzzle-loading rifle took up to fifteen minutes to reload. In case a deer was missed with the first shot he could hardly be expected to wait around while the hunter reloaded his gun. He promptly disappeared, and with him vanished hopes of fresh meat for a hungry family. Either the hunter got his prey with his first shot or he did not get it at all. His first shot was his *only* shot, so he made it his very best.

The disadvantage modern hunters suffer from the repeating gun or the semi-automatic rifle is that it makes for carelessness and inaccuracy. If a rifleman misses with his first shot, he has another and still another that he can squeeze off in seconds. As a result he often shoots recklessly. Seldom does he aim with concentrated desperation because he is aware he has more than one shot in his gun. He develops a deep-seated "I-have-lots-of-chances" attitude. So he may not take good care of his first opportunity.

We would all live more skillfully if we abided by the "only-one-shot" philosophy. Supposing all of us in our town or in America would discard our "automatic-rifle attitude" — acting as if we had a guarantee of innumerable days and years ahead of us, so that if we spoil the present we can still make amends in the tomorrows. Instead, let everyone pretend he has only one day to live. He must make the most of it. He will then soak up the beauties lying unappreciated near him. He will spread around him all the happiness he can, thickly and as far as his influence can reach. He will be outgoing and responsive. He will be cheerful and less critical of his family and friends and even his enemies. He will be loving and forgiving.

Living as if God has given you but one day to live is a way of making all your days happy and meaningful, for yourself and for others.

*Thirty-four*

# GETTING READY TO LIVE

IN ONE WAY, at least, animals seem smarter than human beings. The more highly developed mammals and birds prepare their offspring to face the realities of life better than many human parents do.

The red fox that now hunts deer mice beneath the snows of Hidden Brook learned the arts of stalking and pouncing upon its prey when but a short-legged pup playing on a sunlit knoll outside its natal den. To this hillock home vixen and dog fox brought crippled mice for their lively sons and daughters. These mice had been purposefully maimed by the parent foxes so that they could not elude the pursuit of the agile, but still clumsy, puppies. Tossed before the bouncy, bright-eyed youngsters, the mice tried to get away. But those golden red balls of fluff were upon the mice before they could reach the nearest grass clumps. They were grabbed by tiny jaws and felt the prick of sharp little teeth. The squeaking prey were tossed into the air and rolled and tumbled about while the gay young predators whined and yelped shrilly in excitement. All of this play took place under the alert supervision of the vixen and dog fox, and for a purpose. Parents were preparing their children for life. They were teaching them how to meet one of life's stern demands – the demand for food. Even if they were to do it ever so awkwardly at first, infant foxes must learn how to catch mice, for much of their lives would be spent in doing just that.

In the animal world it is the business of more intelligent creatures to prepare their young for living. Parents inspire the development of their youngsters' hidden capacities and draw out their latencies. Otters are notable swimmers, some of the best in the entire animal kingdom. But young otters do not take to water instinctively. Their mothers must educate them to swim. She coaxes. She teases. Sometimes she tricks her babies into their first swim. Taking them for a swim on her back, where they feel secure and unafraid, she

suddenly ducks out from under them. Then they *must* swim.

Bears, which are clumsy and ungainly-looking, can creep through a forest as quietly as a shadow. Such quietness is not accidental. It is taught. When bear cubs are noisy in the forest, their mother quiets them with a warning growl. If they continue to be loud and boisterous, she cuffs them into obedience. Bears that elude hunters by stealing away from them in unbelievable silence have their mothers to thank. While cubs, they were prepared for a hazardous existence by the wild wisdom of she-bears.

Bird-mothers teach their young to fly sometimes by tantalizing the hungry fledglings with food dropped just out of their reach, so that they must fly to it or go without. This, too, is preparation for adulthood, when wild birds can no longer hope for food to be dropped into their mouths. They must go after it or starve.

In spite of all the present-day literature available on rearing children, and regardless of advances made in the field of child psychology, we parents commonly lack ordinary animal wisdom in child education. We frequently forget that childhood in the human creature, as in the animal kingdom, is a period of preparation for living. And if our children are not taught how to handle life while young and impressionable, they will likely never learn the arts and skills of living at all.

For one thing, we are arresting the development of the next generation by making life too easy for our children. We want them to be strong of character, but we try to remove all obstacles from their paths and all opposition to their desires while forgetting that strength can only be developed as there are loads to lift, burdens to bear, and opposition to push against. Intelligence is often defined by psychologists as problem-solving ability, the power to meet new situations and to master them. Some parents prevent the development of intellectual capacity by going ahead of their children and solving every problem for them. If the problem is money, they dole it out rather than allow the child to earn it. If the problem is excessive timidity, they send the child outdoors to play when company comes so that he won't have to meet strangers. My friend Charlie, when a boy in Louisville, Kentucky, was dreadfully afraid of a neighborhood bully who used to follow him home from school, threatening to beat Charlie to a bloody pulp. Charlie was almost petrified with fear every time he saw the brawler approaching. But he managed to escape. Then one day the bully cornered Charlie and threatened to beat the daylights out of him. This time there was no escape. Charlie had to fight and he did. To his utter amazement he gave the bully the thrashing of his life. So it is with facing life's problems. Only by confronting them can a child learn how conquerable they are and how strong and resourceful he is.

Obedience is a vital part of living. No matter what position we hold in life, someone else will have authority over us, and we shall need to obey or take the dire consequences. A wise parent teaches a child the principle of obedience early, so that he is ready to observe rules and regulations and respect authority later on.

Some time ago a disgruntled schoolteacher handed in her resignation, saying: "In our public schools today the teachers are afraid of the principals, the principals are afraid of the superintendents, the superintendents are afraid of the board, the board members are afraid of the parents, and the parents are afraid of the children, and the children are afraid of nobody." Fear, in the sense of being "scared," is not what we want of our children. But if they are to grow into responsible adults, law-abiding and capable of holding jobs, they must learn to follow rules and obey authority. The best time is when they are young. Parents who are so afraid of offending their sensitive little souls and crippling their emerging little personalities that they cannot bear to frustrate their wills are not preparing offspring for life. They are readying them for serious maladjustment and possible mental disorder. Later in life, when a stubborn mind meets rigid rules and an unyielding society, something gives way. It is usually the mind.

Self-control is another necessity in a complex world where our lives are so mixed up with other lives that no one is free to do entirely as he pleases. A child's personality is not warped when he is taught early to use restraints. He is being fitted and adjusted to a world where he has freedom that is never absolute, but always relative. It is a world where he is at liberty to swing his arms, but that freedom ends where someone else's nose begins. He will have freedom of speech, but that freedom ends where someone else's good reputation begins. He will be unable to walk with hobnail boots over others. If he attempts it, they will destroy him. He will need to control his appetites and desires or his body and mind will be ruined. So the sooner he is taught not to eat all the pie he wants, not to poke or curse everyone who displeases him, the sooner he is taught to perform a few unpleasant tasks every day, the better he is prepared for successful living. As Richard Armour once said:

> "Control of wages, prices, and
> Of goods upon the shelves....
> We'd have no need of laws if we
> Could just control ourselves."

Pampering parents, intent upon making childhood too easy for their offspring, only succeed in making maturity impossible for them. We do this harm in the name of love. Yet if we were our children's worst enemies, we could contrive no more diabolical vengeance than so to maim them mentally and spiritually that they would be incompetent to handle life.

While frolicking in the park one day, little John made friends with a jolly old gentleman sitting on one of the benches. The oldster and the boy carried on a lively conversation. Then suddenly and in a teasing way the old fellow said, "Tell me, sonny, what are little boys good for, anyway?"

John was strangely quiet for a moment and then thoughtfully replied, "Well, I guess we're good to make men of."

Of course that is what little boys and girls are good for. Men and women are made from them. It is the appalling responsibility and the glorious opportunity of parents to do the making.

The best that an intelligent parent can do to express love for a child is to prepare him for the successful management of life.

*Thirty-five*

# ROBINS: WINGED PARTICLES OF GREATNESS

MARCH DAYS are fickle. They begin with bright promises of sunshine, but before noon prankish clouds drop slippery sheets of snow on pavements and sidewalks. March dawns break quietly and peacefully, but within an hour boisterous winds plaster trees and houses, roads and cars, with thick layers of sleet.

March warmth invites over-wintering robins away from the shelter of deep cedar swamps and northward from their Southland resorts. Then capricious winds whistle up a snowstorm to take these early birds by surprise. They huddle and fluff out their feathers, insulating their tender bodies against the cold. They face into the wind and occasionally offer to the world a gloom-shattering, happy song, as if they knew that God and creation are not nearly so well served by groans as by cheer.

Above all else an early returning robin is a symbol of brighter days ahead, a harbinger of hope. No matter how unseasonable the weather may be, no matter how heavy the clouds or severe the storm, he changes the complexion of the day for us. Snow or sleet may be falling fast, but a robin's sharp notes puncture the overcast and let a glimmer of spring shine through. We may have suffered reverses in the weather, but a robin's red breast beats with summer sunshine and gladness and its joyous pulsations echo in our hearts. The sight of a robin makes a difference in a March day.

It is this cheer-bringing capacity of our late-winter friend that convinces me that he is a winged particle of greatness, for what is greatness but a talent for making the world happier and better because we have passed that way?

Someone has defined personality in these radiant terms: "When I met him I was looking down. When I left him I was looking up." That is greatness, no matter where it is found. It is the effect that Christ has had on the world. More than any other person in the world's history, He has invited the world to look up.

If even a lowly robin can draw the world's attention upward and lift many a downcast spirit, so can you, and your ability to do that is one measure of your worth.

*Thirty-six*

# DIETS AND DESTINY

WE ARE NEARING the end of winter, and now the time of deep hunger in the North has arrived. Winter supplies of food have dwindled. The woodland pantry is nearly bare. Easily reached browsings have long since been consumed in crowded deer areas, and only the more inconvenient, hard-to-reach alder and birch twigs and maple tips are now available. I remember one late winter day about this season of the year in 1953 looking out the window of the Miller Cabin on the Thunder Bay River in northeastern Michigan and seeing deer across the stream stretching desperately for tender twigs on trees and shrubs. In that heavily populated deer country the larders of their favorite haunts no longer provided abundant food on the lower shelves. They had to reach, and even then seldom could they obtain their favorite delicacies. More often they had to settle for some less tasty substitute. So it is all over the far North now, just before spring begins.

If whitetail deer could order any one kind of food, acorns would doubtlessly be their choice, and next to the acorns they might select the fruit of the blackgum, or persimmon tree, or perhaps maple, poplar, or witch hazel shoots. But now when supplies are low they will make do with cedar, hemlock, and pine. They must either adjust to scarce supplies or perish.

Rabbits, too, have favorite menus. Carrots, cabbage, lettuce, and parsley rate high. Succulent clover, wheat, oats, and soybeans have a high ranking, too. But now in winter they find none of these. At winter's end all the summer left-overs, such as they were able to find earlier in snow-covered gardens and fields, are gone. So rabbits nibble and gnaw the bark of sumac, dogwood, cherry, apple, and peach trees, making a less palatable food serve when their favorite is unobtainable.

As far as we can discern no creature in the North will use this occasion of scarcity for self-pity. None will rebel. Every-

KOHN

one will adapt himself to the food shortage as well as he can, and where he cannot have the best will make the second-best or tenth-best serve his purpose.

Here is one of the prime differences between lower and higher forms of life. If one of the lower insects cannot find the food it prefers, it will lie right down and die. The *Anthrenps museorum,* a beetle that specializes in eating dead and dried insects, will not choose a second-best food if its favorite rations are not available. It dies. If the snail-eating insect, *Cychrus andrewsii,* cannot find snails, it will not eat aphids or wood, seeds, flour, or sap. It dies. Thus it is with numerous kinds of insects and other low forms of life. They must have their preference or perish. But adaptability seems to increase as forms of life reach higher and higher. If a cat cannot have catnip, it will accept a mouse, a fish, a bird, or a saucer of milk. If a deer cannot find acorns, it will eat sweet-fern or cedar. If a man cannot afford steak, he will resign himself to eating frankfurters.

In areas other than eating, adaption is a sign of high intelligence and great spirit. If a person cannot have the job he wants, he can still make the most of the job he has. If he cannot live where he would like, he can still live nobly and by the highest standards of conduct right where he is. Look carefully enough at some of the successes of history and you will find that once they were failures at what they wanted most. They could not reach it. But when they missed their first aim, they did not let discouragement or self-pity destroy them. Like deer in this time of great hunger, they settled for something other than the choicest items on their menu and made strength of it.

James Whistler wanted to become a soldier. But he failed at West Point because he could not master chemistry. He tried engineering, but that profession did not suit him, or he did not suit that profession. Having a knack for painting, he decided to try that as a life's work and became world-famous in the fine arts. His portrait of his mother is one of the most widely known paintings in the history of art.

Phillips Brooks' early ambition was to be a teacher. Upon graduating from college he launched his career in teaching and found he was a failure. The youngsters made him tired and cross, and he was so humiliated at his lack of control over them that he quit teaching and went into seclusion, refusing to see even his close friends. Then, recovering from the blow, he entered the Christian ministry and became one of America's outstanding preachers, the author of a favorite Christmas carol, "O Little Town of Bethlehem," and finally a bishop of the Episcopal Church.

Joseph did not want to go to Egypt. But when his jealous brothers sold him into slavery and he was delivered to the Egyptian, Potiphar, he made the best of it and at last became prime minister of all Egypt and used his God-given wisdom to save the people of a great region from starvation during a prolonged famine. If Joseph had achieved what he wanted most, a life as a shepherd in his own country, scores of thousands would have starved. He made the most of a second-rate situation.

Not everyone can have what he wants most. Many of us must settle for something less than our favorite item, whether it's cedar when we really want acorns, a medium income when we want wealth, being secretary-treasurer when we want to be president, ailing when we want to be well, or followers when we want to be leaders.

God doesn't demand of anyone that he be a resounding success, nor that he do as well as he would like. But God does expect everyone to do as well as he can with the materials on hand – as does a whitetail deer or a cottontail rabbit.

*Thirty-seven*

# WHAT TO DO WITH THE SHADOWS

THE MORNING is cold – only six degrees above zero by our thermometer, and there is not a gust of wind stirring. But sunlight pours down upon our woods, throwing great shadows across the brilliant, sparkling snow, relieving the radiant whiteness of winter's robe with long ribbons of blue velvet. Every creature that passes this way, red squirrel, rabbit, blue jay, and deer, is followed by a blue ghost of himself drifting along, just behind and under him – his shadow.

These deeper shadows of winter are reasons why I love this season in the North. In summer the shades of trees are somewhat lost amidst the dark-green hues of the forest floor, but in winter, on a bright day, the woods present a study in bright light and dark shading. It is a season when photographers glory in their art, venturing into the nippy out-of-doors to catch on film the sparkle of light on sequin-like snow and to capture in their lenses the phantom shadows of trees and animals, skiers, skaters, iceboaters, hunters, and

fishermen. Now, as at no other season, sun and snow afford opportunities for playing with shadows.

I can well recall taking a junior-high-school course in drawing and hearing the teacher direct the class to sketch wooden balls, cubes, and pyramids from models set before us. Any of the students could draw a ball, cube or pyramid with the help of a compass and ruler. However, in many cases they would not look like ball, cube, and pyramid, but rather like an empty circle, an empty square and an empty triangle. To draw them realistically the fledgling artist had to shade them, showing both light and shadows. Later when we drew fruit, flowers, draperies, and people we had to master the problem of what to do with the shadows. They could not be deleted from the picture. They must be included. What hue and value should they be given? How should they be arranged? How could shadows best be used to show the substance and structure of things? What was the meaning of shadows?

That is a problem everyone has, whether in sketching, in photography, or in treating life realistically – knowing what to do with the shadows that belong in the picture.

Nearly every job has its sunlit side and its shadowy aspects, its happy rewards and its drudgery and disappointments. A measure of contentment can be achieved if the job-holder knows that some shadows belong in the picture, and he accepts them without irritableness or bitterness.

Fellowship is the sunlit side of human relationships and bereavement the shadow side. They are part of the same picture. There would be no grief at parting if we never belonged to each other. But who would wish to live in a world where people could not belong to one another, merely so that grief could be avoided? One of the best uses we can make of grief is to see that it is the long shadow cast by the sunlight of human fellowship, and rather than becoming bitter that we have lost a loved one, be thankful that we could have that dear one to enjoy, even for a little while.

Take any shadow you please and trace it far enough and you will see that it is the dark side of a bright object, pain being the shadow of our wondrous capacity to feel, mistakes being the dark side of our glorious freedom to make choices –

even wrong choices, disagreements being the shaded side of the tremendous variety of opinions that make an interesting world.

God has created a bright world here, and a bright world is bound to have shadows. The beauty of life is in knowing what to do with them.

*Thirty-eight*

# PULLS UPWARD AND DOWNWARD

THESE WINTER NIGHTS seem especially made for pondering. Wintry winds whisper ghost stories to the bare-limbed hardwoods and snow-blanketed evergreens and then playfully moan around the corners of our house and mischievously rattle at our windows. A low, sleepy fire nods and dozes over chunks of maple, birch, and apple wood, and – when the wind tires of its pranks – a thick silence, as quiet as distant stars, engulfs the woodland.

In this cozy place my thoughts wander about as lazily and peacefully as does the long, loose veil of smoke above our chimney. They go to the warm dwellings of raccoons in hollow trees not far from Hideaway House and roam a bit further on to tufts of dry grass that hide small, furry, bright-eyed bodies. They frolic across deep snowdrifts with snowshoe hares, and linger at the woods' edge in friendly communion with whitetail deer that pause in their browsing to look toward our window lights in wonder, lightly touched with fear.

But mostly, just now, my mind whimsically plays with thoughts of how strangely the woodland realm is fashioned by the use of two opposing forces – an upward pull and a downward tug. For instance, around us stand those giant plants, the trees. They persistently climb toward the sky, their branches stretching toward the light. And their little cousins, the shrubs, struggle upward, too, never attaining any towering height, but always reaching up as if seeking some mystical fellowship with the stars. Yet, while their limbs and twigs respond to the upward pull of light from above, the roots of trees and bushes are pulled downward by the tug of gravity and by a deep plant-thirst for ground water. At any given instant a plant is a battleground of two forces – an upward and a downward pull.

That wispy, thin flag of smoke floating above our house,

groping heavenward, rises by force of the heat within it. But then again, before it moves far up into the atmosphere, its innumerable minute particles of ash and unburned specks of wood will float to earth again, becoming part of the soil, some day to be absorbed as food by trees and grasses. Smoke rises. We see that. But it falls to earth again, unseen. Smoke is a sinuous paradox of upward and downward pulling forces.

The very house in which we live aspires upward, like most other houses of our land. Studdings rise. Rafters slope toward the treetops. The roof ascends to a peak that points toward the sky's zenith. This house points heavenward. But it's the downward drag of its weight, the steady earthward pull of gravity that binds the house fast to the whirling world on which it rests. A good house harbors the tensions of its upward and downward pull.

The earthly balance between upward and downward forces is felt in all of us. We have inspirations and aspirations that draw us toward the heights. But we feel gravitational forces within us, too, and they pull us down. And this tension is not always as bad as it first appears.

Look at the self you want to be, and then look at yourself just as you are. The person you aspire to be is a bigger and better person than your actual self. To examine your potential self is to look upward to standards not yet attained and toward ideals not yet realized. To analyze your actual self means facing your shortcomings and failures realistically so that you can know what needs correction. Such introspection demands the sort of perspective that one achieves from a high hill over a village when only the very big things in the town below seem big, and the little things appear very little indeed. This downward look toward oneself brings on dissatisfaction, the kind of wholesome discontent from which all progress is made. A growing soul is one who has a good balance between his upward and downward look.

The grace of humility is a result of a good balance between the upward tug and the downward pull we feel within ourselves. There can be no human virtue without temptation. The person who prides himself on never having the slightest temptation to do wrong is no saint. He is either an unspeak-

ably great liar or a spiritual vacuum. Even Jesus had His forty days in the wilderness of character-testing. A humble reliance upon God arises from our awareness that we are bombarded by testing that we are not supposed to resist with our own strength alone. Like the keystone of an arch, *we stand by our tendency to fall.*

This is Christmastime, and the old, sweet story of the coming of the Bethlehem Babe is as modern as tomorrow's newspaper, for it reminds us once again of the age-old, yet ever new, double lure of the low and high upon us. It tells of an inn with no rooms for a woman with child. It describes King Herod's seeking the whereabouts of the newborn King, pretending he wished to worship Him while he laid plans to kill Him. And it's the story of hundreds thronging the streets drawn on by little affairs, unaware that history was being split into B.C. and A.D. by a Baby's faint cry. Thus, Christmas reminds us of our uncharitableness, our duplicity, our dimness of comprehension, the downward drag of our attentions and loyalties.

But mainly, Christmas is the story of the strange and strong attraction of the good. Christmas means Wise Men irresistibly drawn from the East by the little Babe of Bethlehem. And Christmas means shepherds enticed from their flocks, attracted by the tug of that little Life upon them until they said to one another, "Let us now go even unto Bethlehem and see this thing which is come to pass, which the Lord hath made known unto us."

Well, that's what I am counting upon these days – the pull toward Bethlehem, the attraction Christ still holds for the souls of men. The balance of power that first Christmas night seemed to be pulling the world downward. What chance did that helpless Babe have when pitted against Herod's legions? But the Wise Men believed in the Baby and came from afar to do Him reverence. And common shepherds believed in Him, too, and were drawn to His manger.

In the short view this world belongs to the forces that pull downward. It is Herod's world. But in the long view, the Christmas view, this is God's world, and the lure of the Highest is the strongest pull of all.

*Thirty-nine*

# SOFTENED OUTLINES

NOW WINTER deepens in the North as December days creak past, carrying us ever nearer the year's end. Snow falls heavily from the leaden skies, and prankish winds toss the crystal whiteness into high drifts. Birches, poplars, maples, ash, and elms on our acres are clothed with glistening mica, and the evergreens wear thick, jeweled, woolen robes. Winter's wizardry has cast enchantment over the North Country, teasing Mother Nature until, unnerved, she dropped her jewelry box, spilling sparkling beauty all around.

But even more beautiful than the dazzling whiteness is the new softness one sees everywhere. Roof peaks are rounded by the snow. The sharp needles of spruce, balsam, and pine are cushioned by a white coverlet. Jagged stump tops are capped, and the sharp ends of broken limbs are mittened. Everywhere, in woods, by brookside, or in open field, sharp outlines have yielded to the artful skill and charm of a wintry snowstorm until every object has been attired with a gentle grace.

Human beings, too, lose much of their rough, sharp angularity as December moves toward Yuletide. Much of the beauty of the Christmas season lies in what happens to the human spirit as we draw near Nativity Day. Just as the sharp outlines of roofs, trees, shrubs, and fences soften into flowing elegance under the influence of fallen snow, so the harshness of the soul is touched by the celebration of the Savior's birth.

Even those who are customarily selfish now begin thinking more of others. What they want for Christmas yields to what they will give to dear ones, and the "getters," like the Wise Men, come to Christmas Day "bearing gifts."

The arrogant know-it-alls, positive about all things, find their obstinate certainties giving way under the mystery and wonder of the old story of the Christ Child's coming. Here is one thing that defies their easy, off-hand, self-satisfied explanations. The little King, without a palace, or a crown, or an army, or a sword, or a kingdom, and oppressed by King Herod who sought to murder Him, becomes Sovereign of Souls to millions everywhere. How? Ask any pretentious know-it-all this Christmas season, and, softened by the mystery of the incarnation, he will doubtlessly surprise himself and you with a new-found humility and answer, "I do not know. It is beyond me."

Our rough neglect of the things that matter most is covered now with a new thoughtfulness and awareness of what is beautiful, good, and true. Even the snow seems whiter and purer at Christmas, and the stars seem brighter. Friendships are more cherished. Children are dearer. Husbands and wives become a bit more tender. This is a time of receptiveness, when the opening of gifts and the opening of hearts seem to go together naturally.

While I occasionally hear wild laments about the commercialization of Christmas (and some of the complaints are

justified), still, can anyone point to another period of the year when our natures are so dispossessed of greed, so caught up in beauty, joy, and wonder? Is there ever another day when this sometimes grim, ugly, hard, and sordid world is so overspread with splendor?

Christmas is a good time to see ourselves as we ought always to be. It is a time of kindness and forgiveness, a time of self-forgetfulness and remembrance of others, a season of quiet gratitude, appreciation, and joy in belonging to one another. Christmas envelops us with the spirit that ought always to be ours.

We need now to let Christmas melt on us and run down to the roots of our being, so that we shall be nourished and sustained by that spirit in all our days that lie ahead.

*Forty*

# A NORTHERNER'S PRAYER ON CHRISTMAS EVE

As FLAMES of countless hearths warm the flesh of earth's unnumbered children, and the smoke of limitless fires ascends to greet the friendly stars, so let our hearts glow with cheer and our thoughts leap God-ward at Christmastime.

As the ground's poor rubble of fallen leaves and broken twigs and rotting logs is covered by the clean white snow, so wrap our blunder-littered past in Thy over-spreading love and tender mercy.

As lifeless-looking trees bear sleeping buds that will burst and bloom at last when kissed by spring's warm breath, so may hidden good in us blossom now to Thy enlivening touch.

As spruce and hemlock boughs bend without breaking under heavy snows and later rise again, teach us to bow beneath life's burdens with a grace akin to theirs and then to stand again, strong and straight.

As white-pine limbs obey the merest murmur of winter winds and move to their commands, so may our souls answer to the whisperings of Thy Spirit.

As kindly limbs of evergreens bid cordial welcome to winter birds and shelter them from chill night air, let all Thy children find cover tonight in thoughts of Thy greatness and Thy love.

As Bethlehem's Star shines not alone above David's town tonight, but over every manger and upon all homes and above every land, O God, let not the Christmas joy and peace be mine alone, but everyone's, everywhere. In the Christ Child's name. Amen.